PALEO SMOOTHIES

150 SMOOTHIE RECIPES FOR ULTIMATE HEALTH

MARIEL LEWIS, AMAZINGPALEO.COM

Adamsmedia

Avon, Massachusetts

Published by
Adams Media, a division of F+W Media, Inc.
57 Littlefield Street, Avon, MA 02322 U.S.A.
www.adamsmedia.com

ISBN 10: 1-4405-7465-0
ISBN 13: 978-1-4405-7465-8
eISBN 10: 1-4405-7466-9
eISBN 13: 978-1-4405-7466-5

Printed in the United States of America.

10   9   8   7   6   5   4   3

Library of Congress Cataloging-in-Publication Data

Lewis, Mariel.
  Paleo smoothies / Mariel Lewis, AmazingPaleo.com.
     pages cm
  Includes index.
  ISBN-13: 978-1-4405-7465-8 (paperback)
  ISBN-10: 1-4405-7465-0 (paperback)
  ISBN-13: 978-1-4405-7466-5 (ebook)
  ISBN-10: 1-4405-7466-9 (ebook)
  1. Smoothies (Beverages) 2. Fruit juices. 3. Prehistoric peoples--Food. I. Title.
  TX840.B5L49 2014
  641.87'5--dc23
                            2013047402

Always follow safety and commonsense cooking protocol while using kitchen utensils, operating ovens and stoves, and handling uncooked food. If children are assisting in the preparation of any recipe, they should always be supervised by an adult.

Many of the designations used by manufacturers and sellers to distinguish their product are claimed as trademarks. Where those designations appear in this book and F+W Media, Inc. was aware of a trademark claim, the designations have been printed with initial capital letters.

Cover design by Frank Rivera and Preston Lewis.
Photography by Kelly Jaggers.

This book is available at quantity discounts for bulk purchases.
For information, please call 1-800-289-0963.

Dedication

I dedicate this cookbook to my husband. My rock, my encourager, my inspiration, my best bud, my lover, my world. Honey, this book wouldn't be possible without your support. I love you more than words can explain. You and me, forever.

CONTENTS

INTRODUCTION

Vanilla Coconut Cream Smoothies. Star Fruit Paradise Smoothies. Dandelion Greens Smoothies.

These smoothies sound delicious, right? They certainly are, but there's more to these smoothies than their amazing taste. All of these nutrient-packed drinks are appropriate for the Paleo diet that's taking the world by storm!

In *Paleo Smoothies*, you'll find 150 smoothie recipes full of culinary creativity that nourish your body and satisfy your taste buds! These nutrient-rich and easy-to-make recipes only call for the best smoothie ingredients available, which guarantees an amazing taste and a drink that will feed your body right! In addition, the recipes are broken down into a variety of sections to suit your taste and meet your needs. Some smoothies will crash those cravings for sweets that are common while dieting, some will make you feel more alert, some will get you ready for bed, and some will even take your taste buds on an exotic journey of flavor. Using these sections as a guide, it's easy to choose your own smoothie-making adventure! You'll also learn some smoothie-making basics that will help you master the creation of great-tasting, all-natural smoothie recipes, and you'll see how to apply these lessons to make your own Paleo diet–approved smoothies.

In addition to the deliciously inventive smoothie recipes found in Part 2, you'll also learn invaluable information about how to live the Paleo lifestyle and make it work for you. In Part 1, you'll find information about the Paleo diet, and you'll learn how to make an easy-to-follow plan. What foods can you eat? What should you have in stock in your kitchen to make Paleo smoothies? Why are smoothies an essential part of your Paleo journey? You'll find answers to these questions and more!

Whether you're new to the Paleo diet or you're just looking for some amazingly delicious smoothies to add to your Paleo repertoire, use the detailed information in *Paleo Smoothies* to your advantage and enjoy the success of your very own Paleo journey. Let's toast to you and to your health—with a smoothie of course!

PART 1

Smoothies and the Paleo Diet

Why should I drink smoothies on the Paleo diet?

How can I make sure my smoothies are easy to make and delicious?

What's the deal with the Paleo diet anyway?

You'll learn the answers to these questions and more in this part of the book. If you're looking for information on why the Paleo diet may be good for you, your health, and your overall lifestyle, you'll find it in Chapter 1. You'll also learn the basics of crafting both the smoothies found in Part 2 and your very own smoothie creations in Chapters 2 and 3. Think of smoothie making as an art and these chapters as your paints. You need to know the fundamentals of smoothie making so you can begin the creation of a healthy lifestyle that works for you—without confusion and wasted time. Also, the more you know about smoothies and the Paleo diet, the more they will become a part of your life. You'll be able to translate your skills to healthier smoothie making and Paleo food preparation as well. Knowledge is power, after all!

So take the time to educate yourself about all aspects of Paleo smoothies! After reading these chapters, you should feel confident, well equipped, and ready to get your blender going to make some delicious smoothies for yourself and your family. Gain knowledge on the benefits of smoothies in your diet, know what tools and techniques you should use when preparing your drinks, and understand how to best prepare yourself to make the smoothie-making process a breeze. If you know what you're doing and understand the ins and outs of Paleo smoothies, your smoothie-making experience is sure to be a great one!

CHAPTER 1
Introduction to the Paleo Diet

Congratulations! You're ready to start or have already started living the Paleo lifestyle. But was does that really mean? The Paleo Diet, also known as the Paleolithic Diet, the Caveman Diet, the Stone Age Diet, or the Hunter-Gatherer Diet, was made popular by Walter L. Voegtlin during the mid-1970s. It has been researched, revised, and discussed by many modern authors ever since. This nutritional plan is based on the premise that humans are not meant to eat dairy, grains, legumes, or highly processed foods. Instead, humans should mimic the diet followed by people during the Paleolithic era, an era that lasted 2.5 million years and ended about 10,000 years ago. During this time, the human diet focused on eating high-protein foods (a low-glycemic diet), fruits and vegetables (containing healthy phytochemicals, vitamins, and minerals, which tend to promote proper immune function and make you healthier), and long-chain omega-3 fatty acids (which calm down inflammation).

Now, hunting and gathering in the modern world is a bit too much to ask; realistically, no one has the time, skill, or desire to grab a bow and arrow and go to the woods to try to catch something to eat on a daily basis. However, you are more than able to access all the wonderful foods that cavemen consumed more than 10,000 years ago. You can go to the nearest grocery store and find Paleo staples like beef, chicken, pork, fish, vegetables, fruits, nuts, seeds, and healthy cooking oils. When you live the Paleo lifestyle, you can indulge in the beautifully colored fruits and vegetables found around various parts of the earth, savor the juicy flavors of a nice rib-eye steak or salmon fillet, and munch on raw nuts and seeds. Notice that Paleo foods are not processed; they are all-natural. They are not genetically modified; they are organic. They are not sweetened with high-fructose corn syrup, but rather with raw honey or maple syrup.

Throughout this chapter, you'll find information on how to kick-start your very own Paleo journey, and learn why the Paleo diet is an ideal lifestyle. You'll also discover a few key pointers on how to live the Paleo diet, and determine what you can and cannot eat while living the Paleo lifestyle. Let's dive in and take a look!

How to Live the Paleo Life

Let's start living Paleo! You're committed and want to fully submerge yourself into the wonderful world of Paleo. It's time to learn how to get started. Let's take a look at how you can prepare.

Clean Out Your Pantry

Go through your pantry and refrigerator and use your best judgment to get rid of any products that contain unnatural or processed ingredients. You only want to keep organic proteins, vegetables, fruits, nuts, seeds, and healthy oils. The list of items that need to go in the trash includes things like potato chips, cookies, pancake mix, cereals, crackers, ketchup, mayonnaise, and basically anything that has ingredients that are difficult to pronounce, such as butylated hydroxyanisole, sodium benzoate, and more. You won't need any of these foods while you're on the Paleo journey. While you're at it, organize your pantry and refrigerator so you have a nice, clean space for all the wonderful Paleo-approved foods that you'll use to replace the bad stuff.

Go Paleo Shopping

To successfully follow the Paleo diet, you need to learn how to "shop smart." Take the time to examine the grocery stores close to your home. Figure out where to buy the most affordable and the most colorful fruits and vegetables, the freshest seafood, the crunchiest almonds sold in bulk, the place that imports exotic overseas produce, and so on. It is essential to learn these things when trying to provide the best-tasting and affordable foods for your family. It will pay off in the future. If you don't like to go to grocery stores, you can also buy Paleo foods online. Try sites like LocalHarvest.org, or even a site that's wild and spicy like Latin-Merchant.com.

While you're at your favorite grocery store or browsing your favorite website, take the time to stock up on Paleo pantry must-haves and fresh and organic produce needed for the week. (You'll find lists of approved Paleo foods later in this chapter.) It's a good idea to only buy enough protein and produce to last you one week. By buying once a week, you will keep your veggies, fruits, and protein as fresh and delicious as they can possibly be. You'll get better results with your recipes this way. As you're shopping, spend most of your time perusing the perimeter of the grocery store, where the fresh meats and fresh produce are found, instead of in the pre-packaged food middle aisles. You will find that the majority of

Paleo-friendly foods are found in this section of most grocery stores.

Learn How to Eat Paleo

A great thing about the Paleo diet is that it does not require calorie counting. However, you have to be smart about what to eat and how often to eat. The best way to consume food while following the Paleo diet is to eat smaller meals every three hours. Each meal should contain small portions of protein (fist-size), vegetables (⅔ of your plate), and fruits and omega-3 fatty acids (these two together should make up for ⅓ of your plate). Eating this way will help keep your insulin levels stable, your energy high, and your digestive system in check, all while helping support healthy weight loss, if that's part of your goal.

To stay on track you want to make your food as accessible and quick to put together as possible, and you can do that by preparing your Paleo meals and snacks in bulk ahead of time. This will allow you to have healthy foods available in your kitchen at all times for whenever you and your family get hungry. It will also help you avoid trips to the nearest fast food restaurant, binging on unhealthy processed foods, and making bad food choices altogether. Keeping smoothie ingredients accessible and ready in your kitchen will also ensure that you can whip together a Paleo smoothie in no time flat. Having smoothie ingredients washed, sliced, cubed, frozen, or juiced in your refrigerator ready to be placed in a blender, will cut your smoothie-making time in half. You'll actually be able to prepare delicious and healthy drinks in a matter of minutes! You'll find these methods to be very helpful in your everyday life; they don't take much effort on your part and they will definitely make your Paleo lifestyle a breeze.

Try Paleo-Approved Cooking

This is a fun step! You'll need to get your hands "dirty" and put together wonderful Paleo-approved meals for you and your family. This is where Paleo cookbooks and blogs come into play. There are a lot of great resources out there that have amazing, great-tasting Paleo recipes you can follow, and you can start by trying the Paleo smoothie recipes found in Part 2 of this book. Reading different blogs and cookbooks will provide you with plenty of great ideas, but the smoothies found here will help you make quick and easy Paleo snacks or meals that can help you ease into the Paleo routine. Be sure to vary your menu from week to week and day to day. You don't want to fall off the Paleo diet because you're bored of eating the same foods. Also, as discussed earlier, make sure you get that shopping out of the way early so you have everything you need for your kitchen creations!

Include Your Family on Your Journey

Once you've followed the Paleo diet for a few weeks, you'll realize that it is the best way to eat; you'll feel energetic, have a more regulated digestive system, sleep better, won't feel bloated, and may even lose weight in the process. Since you want only the best for your family, slowly introduce them to your newly learned Paleo ways by letting them help in the kitchen or by letting them try your delicious Paleo smoothies. After all, you want the ones you love to feel as great as you do!

Live an Active and Balanced Life

Join a yoga class, take long walks with your spouse, play with your kids, start a hobby, sleep eight hours every night, socialize, and participate in community events. Of course, eating healthy is extremely important for your health, but there is more to health than healthy food. You need to have a balanced spiritual, mental, and emotional life as well. Take charge and make those changes you know you should make to get you to where you need to be. This is your life; own it and live it!

What to Eat on the Paleo Diet

One of the most difficult things about making any sort of dietary lifestyle change is figuring out what you can and can't eat. You already know that you can't have dairy, grains, legumes, or processed sugars, but what *can* you have? A good rule of thumb is if you are able to grow it, pick it, or hunt it, then you can eat it. Here you'll find some general lists of Paleo ingredients that are broken up by type of food, as well as some of the staples that you should keep in stock at all times. Note that all of the superfood ingredients (foods with amazing and multiple health benefits) that you should have in stock for Paleo smoothies are marked with a ⓢ.

PROTEINS

Note: These need to be organic, grass-fed, and cage-free. Try to consume different protein varieties, as this will help you obtain different nutrients. Try to keep eggs, chicken, turkey, bacon, bison, tilapia, and salmon in your kitchen at all times.

- Poultry
- Beef
- Pork
  - Bacon
- Game meat like bison
- Seafood

FRUITS

Note: Any fruit is allowed, so choose your favorites. Shopping seasonal fruits will make your dollars stretch a bit more and provide you with the juiciest, most colorful fruits. Try to keep avocados, bananas, oranges, apples, grapes, pumpkin, and various organic all-natural fruit juices in your kitchen at all times.

- Açaí
- Apples
- Apricots
- Avocados ⓢ
- Bananas ⓢ
- Blackberries ⓢ
- Black currants
- Blueberries ⓢ
- Cantaloupes

- Cherries
- Coconuts
- Cranberries
- Figs
- Grapes Ⓢ
- Grapefruits Ⓢ
- Honeydew melons
- Huckleberries
- Kiwis Ⓢ
- Lemons Ⓢ
- Limes Ⓢ
- Mangos
- Medjool dates
- Nectarines
- Oranges Ⓢ
- Papayas
- Passion fruit
- Peaches
- Pears Ⓢ
- Pineapples
- Plums
- Pomegranates
- Pumpkin
- Raspberries Ⓢ
- Soursops (guanabanas)
- Squash
- Strawberries Ⓢ
- Watermelons

VEGETABLES

Note: Any vegetable is allowed, so pick your favorites. Choose a wide variety of vegetables to get the best results. Shopping seasonal vegetables will make your dollars stretch a bit more, and will provide you with the most colorful and flavorful varieties available. Try to keep broccoli, kale, spinach, lettuce, watercress, arugula, beets, red cabbage, mushrooms, onions, garlic, cauliflower, cucumbers, asparagus, tomatoes, bell peppers, jalapeño peppers, zucchini, squash, and carrots in your kitchen at all times.

- Artichokes
- Arugula
- Asparagus
- Beets
- Bell peppers
- Broccoli
- Cabbage
- Carrots
- Cauliflower
- Celery
- Chili peppers
- Cucumbers
- Dandelion greens
- Eggplant
- Fennel
- Garlic
- Kale Ⓢ
- Leeks
- Lettuce
- Onions
- Spinach Ⓢ
- Squash
- Swiss chard
- Tomatoes
- Watercress
- Zucchini

TUBEROUS ROOT VEGETABLES

Note: Any tuberous root is allowed, so pick your favorites. Try to include these in your diet frequently, as they provide you with great vitamins and nutrients. Try to keep sweet potatoes, yams, ginger, and cassava in your kitchen at all times.

- Cassava
- Ginger
- Parsnips
- Potatoes
- Radishes
- Sunchokes
- Sweet potatoes Ⓢ
- Taro root
- Turnips
- Yams

FRESH HERBS

Note: Any fresh herbs are allowed, so choose your favorites. Try to keep cilantro, parsley, thyme, basil, rosemary, and mint in your kitchen at all times.

- Basil
- Chamomile
- Chiles
- Cilantro
- Cinnamon
- Dill
- Lavender
- Mint
- Oregano
- Parsley

- Peppermint
- Rosemary
- Sage
- Spearmint
- Sprouts
- Tarragon
- Thyme
- Turmeric

ALL-NATURAL/ORGANIC SPICES

Note: All spices are allowed (with the exception of any that have sugar added), so pick your favorites and build up a good selection to have available in your home. These will be useful to add to your proteins, vegetables, desserts, and smoothies! Try to keep all of the spices on this list in your kitchen at all times.

- Allspice
- Apple pie spice
- Basil leaves
- Black pepper
- Celery flakes
- Chili powder
- Chipotle chili pepper
- Chives
- Cilantro leaves
- Cinnamon
- Coriander
- Crushed red pepper
- Cumin
- Curry
- Dill seed
- Dill weed

- Garlic powder
- Ginger
- Ground cloves
- Ground red pepper
- Ground mustard
- Herbes de Provence
- Nutmeg
- Onion powder
- Oregano
- Paprika
- Parsley leaves
- Pumpkin pie spice
- Rosemary leaves
- Sea salt
- Sesame seeds
- Thyme
- Various Mrs. Dash spices

NUTS

Note: All nuts, except peanuts (which are legumes), are allowed, so choose your favorites. Nuts must be consumed in moderation. They're great for homemade trail mix, salad toppings, dessert toppings, and Paleo flours and butters. Try to keep the following in your kitchen at all times.

- Cashews
- Hazelnuts
- Macadamia nuts
- Pecans
- Slivered blanched almonds Ⓢ
- Walnut halves Ⓢ
- Whole almonds Ⓢ

SEEDS

Note: All seeds are allowed, so pick your favorites. Try to keep the following in your kitchen at all times.

- Chia seeds
- Flaxseeds Ⓢ
- Pumpkin seeds
- Sesame seeds
- Sunflower seeds Ⓢ

OILS

Note: Natural plant oils (such as nut oils, seed oils, olive, and some fruit oils) are great for a wide variety of dishes in your Paleo kitchen. Pick your favorite plant oils for frying, baking, sautéing, and dipping/dressings/marinades. Try to keep the following in your kitchen at all times.

- Avocado oil (for frying and sautéing)
- Coconut oil (for frying, sautéing, and baking)
- Flax oil (for dressings)
- Extra-virgin olive oil (for sautéing, dressings, dipping, and marinades)
- Sesame oil (for frying and sautéing)
- Walnut oil (for dressings, dipping, and marinades)

MISCELLANEOUS

Note: These ingredients will make your Paleo journey a bit more enjoyable, but you should eat them in moderation. Try to keep the following in your kitchen at all times.

- Almond butter
- Almond extract
- Baking powder
- Baking soda
- Cacao nibs (dark chocolate) Ⓢ
- Canned coconut milk
- Coconut butter
- Coconut powder
- Herbal teas (you can have as many herbal teas as you like) Ⓢ

- Organic maple syrup
- Raw honey
- Unsweetened almond milk
- Unsweetened cacao powder
- Unsweetened coconut flakes
- Unsweetened shredded coconut
- Vanilla extract

Again, you can use most of the afore-mentioned Paleo ingredients to prepare the delicious Paleo smoothies in Part 2. Also, try to keep a variety of organic, fresh fruit/veg-etable juices, pulps, and extracts in stock to make your smoothies extra tasty. You'll be glad you did!

CHAPTER 2

Why Drink Smoothies on the Paleo Diet?

As you know, living the Paleo lifestyle means eating the most natural foods available in the market and consuming all organic goods that have not been processed or genetically modified. This way of eating keeps your body functioning properly; you don't ingest man-made ingredients nor added hormones, so your body can easily and more rapidly process foods to acquire energy. But even though the Paleo diet is very "clean" (100 percent all natural), your body does need a break from digesting all meals. The Paleo smoothies found in Part 2 help your body detox, boost your immune system, help with digestion, and much more! Adding smoothies to your Paleo lifestyle can provide you with a wonderful break and help you detox from all those unwanted pollutants you've had a hard time getting rid of on your own. Drinking nutritious liquids will help you flush a lot of the bad stuff out . . . naturally! In this chapter, you will learn *exactly* how Paleo smoothies can benefit your body, and you'll gain a better understanding of the wonderful effects that these nutritious liquids can have.

Before you read on, please note this important tip: You don't have to add a smoothie to your diet every day, and you shouldn't stress about the days when you can't swap a smoothie in for a meal. If you can, you'll receive all the wonderful benefits discussed here. If not, just try again tomorrow! You don't need to follow a strict health regimen when it comes to smoothies. Instead, just do your best to embrace the great effects fresh smoothies have on your overall health.

So what do Paleo smoothies bring to the table? Let's take a look!

They Cleanse and Detox

A lot of people who follow the Paleo diet already eat very clean diets that include many vegetables, fruits, and organic proteins. If this sounds like you, you may think that you don't need to detox and cleanse because you already eat very clean. However, this isn't necessarily true. You're not just exposed to toxins through the foods you put in your body, but also from environmental pollution ranging from chemicals in your cleaning supplies to fertilizers used in farms that grow foods you consume. In addition, those few "cheat meals" that you may squeeze into your Paleo diet to help combat cravings may contain toxins. So why is it important to cleanse? When your body is highly toxic and imbalanced, you may find that you experience headaches, bad skin, constipation, allergies, bad breath, and more. By giving your body smoothies packed with all-natural and top-quality fruits, vegetables, and healthy fats, you take action to help your colon, kidneys, and liver combat toxins and fluid imbalances.

Consuming liquids rather than solids gives your body a break and has a cleansing effect on your colon. By substituting one of your solid meals with liquids once a day (or even once a week), you allow your system to flush out residues from solids consumed earlier (in the day or week). Sometimes, undigested foods can cause the colon to produce a mucus-like buildup, which can create toxins that can slowly poison your body. Think of drinking smoothies as running fresh water down a partially clogged pipe; a nice flushing will allow the pipe to flow smoothly, and will reduce the chances of it clotting and collapsing. Your colon can resemble this tired thin pipe if it's not properly cared for. Substitute a solid meal with a nice smoothie for preventative maintenance and to keep it running the way it's meant to run.

Your colon isn't the only organ that smoothies can help detox; your kidneys and liver can benefit as well. Your liver is constantly trying to eliminate undesired bacteria and toxins that come from contaminated foods and the general contamination in your surroundings. Your kidneys try to keep your body in balance when it's overloaded with minerals like salt. Paleo smoothies will help you detox your liver and kidneys due to the wonderful nutritional composition of the smoothie ingredients themselves. Key ingredients that will help you do this include citrus fruits, cranberry juice, apple juice, pineapple juice, avocados, cucumbers, cilantro, leafy greens, flaxseeds, and more. These smoothie ingredients work as wonderful diuretics, which will help you release toxins that you may be holding on to, and help alkalize your system. By nourishing your organs with Paleo smoothies, you'll become your body's own superhero! Doesn't that sound great?

They Improve Your Digestion

Your digestive system is very responsive; it responds well to healthy and balanced diets, and poorly to unhealthy and unbalanced diets. Simple concept, right? However, your digestive system is not so easy to control.

There are various things that may throw your digestive system off balance. Your diet may lack important fibrous foods and water, you may consume unwanted and unhealthy fats and processed foods, you may chew your food while walking, or you may not provide your body with a good balance of important macros (protein, carbohydrates, and fats). All of these things can easily throw your digestive system off balance. How can you fix this? Drink smoothies!

A quick and easy way to turn things around and kick-start your digestive health is to replace these bad things with smoothies. Not only are smoothies hydrating, they provide lots of great fibrous vegetables and fruits, healthy fats, and filtered water that help with proper digestion. It's a fast and easy solution, especially if you have a busy schedule. Jump on the smoothie bandwagon and forget about bad office snacking and poor digestion!

They Boost Your Immune System and Keep You Strong

You've heard the saying "an apple a day keeps the doctor away," right? Well, the same can be said about many of the nutritious ingredients used to make the Paleo smoothies found in Part 2. You see, the fruits and vegetables packed into these recipes have many essential nutrients that benefit your body and boost your immune system. Vitamins and minerals play hundreds of roles in your body and help to promote a good balance and harmony

in your immune system. Each vitamin is essential to develop and maintain important aspects of proper immune function, whether that be supporting healthy cell function or the release of antibodies from B-cells, promoting T-cell activity, or supporting a sound anti-inflammatory response. Minerals perform a similar job, mostly aiding proper T-cell function and fighting against antibodies. Both vitamins and minerals are present in fruits and vegetables, which is why it is very important to consume a variety.

The good news is that fruits and vegetables are easily accessible and they truly taste amazing. You can eat these in salads, by themselves, or drink them in juice or smoothie form. Smoothies tend to be fun, allowing for an unlimited variety of ingredient combinations, and they pack a nice nutritional punch! The Paleo diet calls for a high consumption of vegetables and a nice intake of fruits, and giving these to your body in smoothie form is the best way to go. You can add large amounts of greens and a nice combination of fruits (and nuts!) to a blender; these will break down nicely and you won't feel like you have to chew for days to get a good amount of nutrients in your body. Your smoothie will not only taste amazing, but you'll be obtaining wonderful amounts of needed minerals and vitamins to boost your immune system.

Furthermore, after an intense workout, hike, run, walk, bike ride, or even a tough work day, you'll likely be tired and low on basic nutrients, and drinking a smoothie will help you maintain a balanced immune system. By making your own all-natural smoothie and adding ingredients such as pumpkin, eggs, nuts, or seeds, that contain good amounts of protein, you'll replenish your nutrient, vitamin, mineral, and protein supplies, and recover properly. You can optimize the results of your workout when you add a protein smoothie thirty to forty-five minutes after a workout. During that period, your muscles are at an optimal protein absorption level. Over time, you'll see an increase in muscle health and strength. With a nice post-workout smoothie, you'll increase your fitness performance, recover faster, and feel more energetic. By providing your body with necessary nutrients on a daily basis, you'll keep your body functioning at its best and your immune system will continue to stay in tip-top shape, keeping you as healthy as can be. A fueled body often gets further in life. So fuel yourself with a post-workout Paleo smoothie instead of reaching for a processed protein bar that is filled with artificial ingredients and who knows what!

your morning class, this rush may force you to skip the most important meal of the day: breakfast. Breakfast is actually the most crucial meal of the day, and by skipping it, you definitely set yourself up for a rough morning. You see, most people sleep six to eight hours each night, and during those hours your body isn't given any nutrition whatsoever. Breakfast gives your body the after-sleep nutrition it needs to kick-start your metabolism, sustain energy throughout the day, and provide essential vitamins that help keep your brain working properly. The same concept goes for lunch and dinner. Don't skip meals; find easy and fast ways to get those meals in.

Fortunately, smoothies are a great way to get the nutrition you need quickly and easily. Choose a recipe and throw the required ingredients in your blender. Two to five minutes later, you're out the door with your smoothie in hand! In addition, smoothies are delicious, and with all the variations found in Part 2, you'll never get bored! With smoothies, you do not sacrifice taste or nutrition. Ever. It's a win-win!

They Give Your Body Quick Nutrition

You may feel that you have little to no time for a healthy meal in the morning. Whether you're getting the kids ready for school, showering and rushing out the door for work, or oversleeping and running late for

They're a Great Snack

You learned how to substitute a smoothie for a meal if time is tight, but smoothies are also great to drink between meals as delicious and easy snacks. If you find yourself hungry before your Paleo dinner is ready, and you need something—and something soon—just prepare a small, 8-ounce smoothie or share a good-size smoothie with someone else. It will calm your hunger and cravings, and keep you full and content until you're able to sit down to your next meal.

Smoothies make a great snack, not only because of the amazing nutrition you get, but also because of how easy and fast they are to whip up. There is nothing like consuming a light Paleo snack in between meals, or in place of a meal if you feel that your body has had enough for the day. Having a smoothie as a snack makes for a wonderfully healthy option while following the Paleo diet. You see, most Paleo diets are high in heavy animal protein, which is difficult for the body to digest, so providing essential nutrients to the body in liquid form lessens your digestive system's workload. Also, if dinner is ready before you finish your smoothie snack, just put the smoothie in the refrigerator and save it for later. It'll stay fresh for one day, so keep calm and smoothie on!

They Cut Down Your Grocery Bill

Do you ever go to the grocery store and buy a ton of fruits and vegetables thinking that you'll eat them all before they go bad? It's a common Paleo problem! Once you start making delicious smoothies, your fruits and vegetables will never go to waste again. As soon as you see your ingredients start to brown or see that they are "mature," you can either throw them in a blender to make a smoothie or freeze them in a zip-top bag to use for future smoothies. How great is that? You won't waste your money by buying food that you'll just throw away, and you'll have frozen, all-natural fruit ready to create those yummy frozen smoothies. Problem solved! Just be sure to keep zip-top bags on hand at all times for freezing purposes.

So What Now?

Paleo smoothies have a large array of benefits; they cleanse and detox your body, they improve your digestion, they boost your immune system and keep you strong, they provide your body with quick nutrition, they serve as a great snack, and they can even help you cut down on your grocery bill. So now that you've learned exactly how Paleo smoothies nourish your body and help you stay healthy, you may be wondering where to begin and what to do next. We'll, you're in the right place! Let's take a look at best practices for Paleo smoothie making!

CHAPTER 3

Be Paleo Smoothie Ready

Are you looking forward to crafting your Paleo smoothie creations? Of course you are! Your taste buds will savor combinations they've never experienced before, your glasses will carry the most beautiful colored drinks, and your health will be taken to a whole new level of greatness! This chapter will equip you with the knowledge you'll need to get started with your Paleo smoothie adventure. You will find suggestions on things like ideal smoothie-making kitchen tools, what top-class smoothie ingredients to use, and tips on how to be smoothie ready at all times. Are you excited? Then read on!

Have the Right Equipment

There are specific tools that you should have on hand to make the smoothie-building process a breeze. If you don't have some of the recommended tools, don't worry—they're not mandatory, and there are substitutes you can use (for the most part) to get the same or similar results. However, owning the tools discussed here will benefit you in two ways.

1. You'll save time: There are particular tools that are optimal for specific purposes, and they do an amazing job of getting the job done. The right kitchen tools will help ensure that the smoothie-making process goes as quickly as possible.

2. You'll use as much of the ingredient at hand as possible: Some of the tools in this chapter are made solely to extract juice from fruits or to strip the skin, peel, or leaves from certain fruits and vegetables, which will in turn maximize your valuable ingredients.

But while you don't need to own every tool on the list, there is one key tool that you will absolutely need: a blender! There are a lot of fantastic and very powerful blenders out there, and it seems like better models are released every year. You don't have to buy the most advanced blender on the market, but the more powerful the blender you have, the better, as you will be blending ice and frozen ingredients that are hard to break down. This is the one tool to splurge on if you can. If you don't currently own a blender, take the time to compare brands and models and read reviews. After all, if you're going to spend a good amount of money on a product, you better know exactly what you're getting. And that research might help you get a great deal on price to boot!

If you have an older blender that you just can't give up, or if you simply don't want to go out and buy a new one, don't worry. You will still be able to make smoothies, just be prepared to keep your blender going for longer periods of time. The more powerful the blender, the faster your drinks will become smooth.

So let's get started! Here is the list of recommended tools, broken down by category:

ELECTRICS

- **Blender:** A key tool for making smoothies and a must-have for all of the recipes featured in this cookbook. If you're looking for top-of-the-line equipment, the Vitamix blender is highly recommend. Even though it is pricier than other blenders, it makes the smoothie-making process a breeze! The Vitamix is very powerful (making your drinks extra smooth), it is easy to clean, easy to store, and it is one of the least noisy blenders on the market. However, there are a lot of options out there when it comes to blenders and you can get great ones

for reasonable prices. Go online and compare blenders by reading product descriptions and reviews; you are sure to find the right fit for you!

- **Food processor:** An all-time Paleo diet favorite due to its versatility. Handles slicing, chopping, mixing, and shredding. It's dishwasher safe and easy to clean. Use it to mix ingredients in a quick manner, or to make your own homemade nut flours and homemade seed and nut butters.
- **Juicer:** A fresh fruit and vegetable extractor. Processes foods efficiently to obtain key nutrients and vitamins, while disposing of unwanted pulp. Great for all kinds of produce.
- **Tea kettle:** Allows you to boil water in a jiffy to make your favorite organic herbal-blend teas. You can use all-natural floral and citrus iced teas instead of water in your smoothies to add in wonderful, refreshing flavors.

GENERAL CUTLERY

- **Citrus knife:** A serrated blade that slices all citrus fruits smoothly. Ideal for oranges, lemons, limes, and grapefruits.
- **Classic produce knife:** Great for preparing larger fruits and vegetables with thick rinds. Has a longer blade that helps you cut all the way across large fruits and a straight edge that makes it easy for chopping. Ideal for tropical fruits such as pineapple, papaya, and watermelon.

- **Cutting board:** These come in a variety of shapes and in various materials. An antibacterial cutting board with a perimeter is recommended because this allows you to contain any juices produced by cutting fruits and vegetables. Make sure it is dishwasher safe.
- **Kitchen shears:** Use for things like opening packages, slicing dried fruits, and cutting fresh herbs.
- **Mandoline slicer:** A very precise and sharp tool to help you slice multiple fruits and vegetables; you can pick how thick or thin you want your slices to be. Ideal for slicing any produce quickly. This is a very sharp tool, so please use it very carefully.
- **Slicing knife:** A knife with a sharp razor and a nice point that produces a clean slice on produce. Ideal for apples and pears.
- **Utility knife:** A multipurpose knife with a sharp blade that is great for both rough and soft foods. Ideal for ingredients like berries and soft skin vegetables.
- **Vegetable knife:** Optimal for trimming, chopping, and slicing vegetables. Works great for fruits as well.

FRUIT TOOLS

- **Apple slicer:** A simple and easy way of getting your fruit quickly sliced. One downward push and voilà, apple cored and sliced!
- **Avocado cuber:** A fantastic tool to scoop out your avocado. It is quick and maximizes fruit extraction.
- **Banana slicer:** Saves time and effort when you need to make uniform banana slices (to top smoothies and such).
- **Cherry pitter:** A wonderful tool that removes cherry pits, helping you save lots of time. Usually dishwasher safe and kid-friendly!
- **Citrus juicer:** A tool that will help you get the last drop from any juicy fruits. Just cut your limes and lemons in half, place one half at a time in the citrus juicer, and you've got yourself lots of good juice to add to your smoothies.
- **Mango pitter:** A tool that slices each mango down the middle and cuts the pit out perfectly.
- **Orange juicer:** An inverted press, just like the citrus juicer, designed specifically for oranges.
- **Peach pitter and slicer:** Very similar to an apple slicer. One easy stroke and you get immediate peach slices from a whole fruit.
- **Pineapple slicer and dicer:** An ingenious tool that helps core, slice, and dice a pineapple in two simple steps, maximizing the use of the fruit. You will also save a lot of time; pineapples can be tricky to cut.
- **Strawberry huller:** A fantastic strawberry-specific tool to help you quickly and easily remove leaves and stems.

VEGETABLE TOOLS

- **Multi-chopper:** An ideal option to chop an army of vegetables (and fruits too), ranging from carrots, to apples, to celery—all at the same time.
- **Vegetable brush (or scrubbing gloves):** A good little kitchen helper; used to rub your vegetables to get them clean. Ideal for sweet potatoes and carrots.

HERB TOOLS

- **Herb mill:** A nice tool to help mince your favorite herbs in a matter of seconds. Ideal for herbs such as rosemary, mint, and oregano.
- **Herb saver:** An innovative tool that allows you to keep your herbs fresh for up to three weeks. No more wasting your beloved cilantro, mint, or rosemary.
- **Herb shears:** Typically smaller than regular kitchen shears. These sharp blades are ideal for finely cutting your favorite herbs and small edible flowers.

ESSENTIAL COOK'S TOOLS

- **Citrus zester:** A great zest scraping tool. Ideal for citrus fruits (limes, lemons, oranges, and grapefruit), ginger, garlic, and nutmeg.
- **Colander or strainer:** A fine mesh that is great for draining fresh fruits, vegetables, and herbs. Ideal for washing your greens, berries, grapes, cilantro, etc.

- **Digital food scale:** A tool to help you measure ingredients accurately. Great to have when a recipe calls for ounces instead of cups.
- **Grater:** A great shredding tool. Dishwasher friendly and easy to use. These can be very sharp, so please be careful when handling.
- **Measuring cups:** Classic measuring utensils. These tools will help you measure the right amounts of each ingredient any smoothie recipe calls for. Great to measure both liquids and powders.
- **Measuring spoons:** This tool will help you measure the right amounts of each ingredient any smoothie recipe calls for. Great to measure liquids and powders.
- **Peeler:** Features a sharp stainless-steel blade that peels produce efficiently. Very easy to use. Ideal for ingredients such as apples, sweet potatoes, carrots, and cucumbers.

MISCELLANEOUS

- **Mason jars with lid:** Helpful for storing opened cans of pumpkin purée or coconut milk. Also great to use as a smoothie glass.
- **Small pan with lid:** A great cookware piece. You can use it to boil eggs, an occasional smoothie ingredient.
- **Straws:** Makes smoothie drinking a whole lot more fun! Choose your favorite colors and shapes.

- **To-go smoothie containers:** Ideal to bring with you to work, to school, or while shopping. You'll find a variety of sizes, shapes, and colors; pick what best fits your needs.
- **Zip-top bags:** A fantastic way to store fruits, vegetables, and herbs. You can either freeze or refrigerate ingredients when placed in zip-top bags. It's a good idea to first wash and slice/cube your produce before freezing; that way it's ready to throw in a smoothie directly from the freezer.

Cooks are empowered in the kitchen by having wonderful equipment available. It seems like there is a tool for every job. Because you lead a busy life, consider taking all the help you can get from these kitchen tools.

Have Ingredients on Hand

Do you feel like there's a prescription for everything nowadays? When you feel tired, take this. When you feel blue, take that. It's always a quick fix—and an expensive one, too! Fortunately, you don't need to take pills or supplements to look, feel, and *actually* stay healthy. The Paleo smoothies found in Part 2 give you a much healthier and less expensive way to achieve those same results.

The adage "you are what you eat" is absolutely true. What you put in your body affects your entire being. It is important that you feed yourself consciously, providing your system with nothing less than a variety of whole, all-natural foods. By eating a diverse, Paleo-friendly mix of fruits, vegetables, roots, seeds, nuts, herbs, and eggs, you can supply your body with all the macronutrients and micronutrients you need to stay strong and healthy. The smoothie recipes in this book work to make each sip count by packing in as many superfoods as possible. Why? Because you can easily throw five to six superfoods into the blender at a time and get a delicious drink that will give you sustained energy, keep you satisfied and full, and feed your body, all at the same time. It's the easiest way to consume lots of nutrients at once. In Chapter 1, you saw several lists of Paleo ingredients that are perfect for smoothies. Go back and take a look at those lists to see which Paleo superfood smoothie ingredients you should keep handy in your kitchen at all times. After all, you can't use what you don't have!

Again, don't ever underestimate the power of providing your body with nutritious ingredients. They will help boost your immune system, improve digestion, and feed your body right! They function as "preventative maintenance" for your body, and making smart choices now will help you prevent problems in the future. You'll be happy you did!

Stay on Track

As you can see, it's worthwhile to start including superfoods in your smoothies. Have a Paleo smoothie every day or once a week; create a routine! In this section, you'll learn about making smoothies a habit. But how can you get started right now? Well, if you're ready and want to make this commitment, here are a few guidelines that can help you stay organized and prepared as you ease into this wonderful health routine.

Use a High-End Blender

You read about using high-end blenders earlier in this chapter, but it really is key. The better your blender is, the better your Paleo smoothies will turn out. A powerful blender will break down all frozen ingredients and ensure that every solid turns into pure liquid very quickly, which allows all of your ingredients to mix well. Also, the better your blender, the faster your smoothies will be ready. When you're making a smoothie, you're likely hungry, and when you're hungry, you don't want to wait around for your blender to break down frozen fruits. To avoid any wasted time and frustration, and to ensure a smooth, well-blended drink, remember that a good blender does the trick—and it does it quickly! You can keep your blender working at its best by following these tips:

- **Boost its flow:** The order in which you add ingredients to the blender is important, as it allows for an easier blending flow. The preferred formula of adding ingredients to the blender is as follows:

  1. Liquids (water, juice, oil, etc.)
  2. Frozen produce
  3. Powders or spices
  4. Ice
  5. Fresh produce

- **Cut produce into smaller pieces:** The smaller the pieces of fruits or vegetables you feed to the blender, the easier it'll be for those to be broken down by the blades once you turn the blender on.

- **Don't leave any chunks behind:** Once you believe every solid has been broken down and all ingredients have mixed appropriately, remove the blender jar from the blender's motor, open its lid, and move the smoothie around to see if any small chunks of fruit are still hanging around. If there are some left, just quickly blend your smoothie for another minute or so. If your smoothie is chunk-free, pour it into your favorite glass and enjoy!

- **Clean your blender right away:** Once you're done using the blender, be sure to clean it immediately. If you let it sit dirty for long periods of time, the blender might collect bacteria, and as the ingredients harden, it might be more difficult to clean. Clean your blender by:

1. Adding dishwashing soap and water to your blender jar and closing its lid.
2. Turning the blender on for a few seconds.
3. Removing the blender jar; rinse and let dry.

So easy, right?

Clean Your Kitchen and Tools

As you'll do with your blender, you want to clean your kitchen and tools right away. The easiest thing to do is to place all dirty tools and gadgets in the dishwasher (if they're dishwasher safe). If they're not dishwasher safe, just go ahead and wash them by hand and let them dry by your blender.

Save Ingredients That Weren't Used

As you clean your tools and kitchen, stow away any unused ingredients. Store any powders, oils, nuts, and seeds back in your cupboards, and refrigerate or freeze any produce leftovers.

Replenish Used Ingredients for Future Smoothies

After you're done cleaning and storing unused ingredients, make a list of all the ingredients you ran out of. Keep your list handy and visible, so you can pick up everything you need the next time you go to the store. If you struggle to make lists, get a grocery list pad that can help you stay organized.

Plan Ahead

It's important to have all the ingredients your smoothie recipes call for, as well as the kitchen tools needed, on hand. If you know you're going to want to make a Banana Almond Smoothie (see Three-Ingredient Smoothies in Part 2) in the morning, you better make sure you have almonds and bananas in your home. Otherwise, your smoothie plans might just have to change altogether in the A.M. Be on top of your grocery list needs; consider it your pre-smoothie homework.

Also, if you do have all the right ingredients for the Paleo smoothies you plan to create, make sure that you've done what you need to prepare them. Some recipes will call for chilled canned coconut milk or frozen bananas, so be sure to plan for all of those requirements. You'll be doing yourself a favor, as the quality of the smoothie may depend on these ingredient preparations.

Remember, Fresh Is Best

Buy everything fresh and, if you can, organic. It's amazing how much more flavorful and juicy organic fruits and vegetables are. There's just no comparison. Organic is always best. Your local farmers' market might carry a lot of the organic produce you need, and their prices are usually a little cheaper than prices at chain stores, so that's always a fabulous option. Also, when you buy produce at the farmers' market, you support local farms and the overall local economy, creating more jobs and sustaining production.

In addition to buying fresh, you also want to freeze your own fruits. By doing this, you know where the frozen goods are coming from, and you're guaranteed that your smoothies don't contain any additives whatsoever.

Buy in Bulk

This is huge. If you go directly to a wholesaler and buy things such as organic nuts, organic seeds, coconut products, cacao powder, and honey in bulk, you'll end up saving a lot of money. When buying in bulk, try to purchase ingredients that will last a few months; that way, you won't have to worry about going through them quickly to prevent them from going bad. If you do buy fresh produce in bulk, be sure to leave out

what you're going to use for that week and freeze the rest in zip-top bags or sealed containers. If you buy things like nuts and seeds, make sure that when you do open them, you store what you don't use in a tightly sealed container. They'll stay fresh and crispy for a long time this way. You can buy bulk items from Costco Wholesale, BJ's Wholesale Club, Cash & Carry, the bulk section at organic grocery stores, and from various online wholesalers and retailers.

Keep Key Nonperishable Items in Stock

In addition to having a good stock of nuts, seeds, and produce at home handy for your smoothies, it's important to keep a decent stock of nonperishable items such as spices, oils, and powders, like cacao and nut flours. These ingredients won't last forever, but they will last you anywhere from six months to one year if they're kept in nicely sealed containers and in controlled temperatures. (The ideal temperature to store these ingredients is room temperature, at 70°F.) Some items should be kept neatly organized in a pantry or in your kitchen cabinets. For example, try keeping a shelf for spices; a shelf for unopened nut flours, nut and seed butters, and cacao powder; a shelf for oils; a shelf for teas; and a shelf for natural sweeteners. The rest of these items—including unsweetened shredded coconut,

coconut flakes, cacao nibs, and opened nut and coconut flours—should be kept in the refrigerator.

Buy Reusable Plastic Smoothie Cups

Generally, enjoying a particular drink depends on the type of glass it's served in. When drinking a smoothie at home, you might use a tall, clear glass with a straw—something that allows a nicely chilled and colorful smoothie to shine. When drinking a smoothie out and about, you may prefer a tall plastic glass with a straw and a cover.

To make sure your smoothie experience is as easy and enjoyable as possible, pick up a few plastic smoothie glasses. You can purchase affordable cups at T.J.Maxx or similar stores; they'll typically have around ten or more different designs to choose from. These glasses are easy to wash and easy to carry, and they make it easy to drink smoothies. It's nice to have a few available at home; that way, every member of your family can take a Paleo smoothie to go!

Incorporate Smoothies Into Your Routine

Earlier in this chapter, you read a bit about making Paleo smoothies a habit, but it's so important that it bears repeating. If you want all the great benefits that these smoothies bring, you have to add smoothies into your daily or weekly meal plans. It's as simple as that!

If you don't have a ton of time in the morning to prepare breakfast, then use that to your advantage and drink your smoothies then. If you struggle to prepare dinner, then drink your smoothies then. If Sunday afternoons are the only days you have time to experiment in the kitchen, then Sundays are when you should drink your smoothies.

Figure out what works best for you and create smoothie-drinking routines around it. If you do this, Paleo smoothies will soon become a habit for you, and you'll even begin to crave your smoothie-drinking time. Humans are creatures of habit; you'll see how quickly you adjust to incorporating more smoothies in your diet if you start scheduling them into your agenda. Give it a try!

Notice How Paleo Smoothies Make You Feel

Pay attention to how you feel after drinking each Paleo smoothie. You'll want to create a mental note of how your body reacts to different ingredients. Track things like your energy, focus, and digestion. By noticing which smoothie combinations your body reacts best to, you will be able to understand what your nutritional needs are. For example, if you feel that your digestion and energy are enhanced after drinking the Honeybunches Smoothie (see "Refreshing Smoothies" section in Part 2), it is probably because your body needs the vitamin B, vitamin C, and fiber that this smoothie has to offer. The more you get to know your body, the better you'll be able to tailor your diet to its needs, ensuring optimal performance and nutrition.

Make Smoothies Fun

There is nothing better than enjoying life and having great experiences, so why not make drinking smoothies fun, too? It'll encourage you to enjoy yourself and get motivated to make Paleo smoothies work for you. Do what you can to get other people excited and involved in the smoothie-making process. Not sure where to start? Try some of the following tips:

- Plan a weekend smoothie-making party with your family and friends. It can be an activity that fills the whole morning. Just grab some friends, go out together, and shop for the best produce you can find. Then go back to someone's house, wash and dry your produce, prepare your tools, and blend away. Have each person make a different smoothie, and share them to see what tastes best.
- Blend a nice cold smoothie after a long football, baseball, or basketball game.
- Have smoothie dates with your workout buddy after the gym.
- Bring a large smoothie with you when going for a hike to keep you hydrated and cool.
- Prepare holiday-themed smoothies for breakfast; blue on the Fourth of July, green on Saint Patrick's Day, red on Christmas morning, etc.
- Play a "guess what's in this smoothie" game with your kids.
- Add interesting fruit and vegetable finds to your drinks and embrace your adventurous self. You may find your new favorite fruit or vegetable this way; you never know!
- Have "Smoothie Sundays" or a "Movie and Smoothies" date planned once a month with your significant other.

The possibilities are endless, so make it fun!

PART 2

The Paleo Smoothies

You've reached the part of the cookbook you've been waiting for! In this part, you'll find 150 Paleo smoothies divided up by smoothie types. You'll find recipes for refreshing smoothies, cleansing smoothies, and energizing smoothies, in addition to green smoothies, three-ingredient smoothies, dessert smoothies, and much more! All of the smoothies in this book are filled with nutritious ingredients that work for the Paleo diet, and each smoothie recipe includes a description of the smoothie itself, the preparation time, preparation difficulty, recipe yield, ingredient list, preparation instructions, serving size, and nutritional content, so you know exactly what you're drinking and how long it'll take to put together.

In addition to being delicious and nutritious, you'll find that the recipes in this part will empower you with the ingredient-combination knowledge you'll need to come up with your very own Paleo smoothie creations in the future. Mixing ingredients and knowing how well they work together is an art. Practice that art by following these recipes, learning from the tips and tricks you've read about, and recognizing what fruits and vegetables mix well together. Once you start testing these smoothies in your own kitchen and tasting them with your family, smoothie-making will become second nature to you, and you'll find yourself mixing and matching your own favorite ingredients in no time! You can even customize your smoothies as you follow the recipes. For example, if you find that your smoothie is too thick, feel free to add a splash of water. If your smoothie is too watery, feel free to add an ice cube or two. It's all about what works for you. Enjoy!

Refreshing Smoothies

Have you ever had a craving for something that can help replenish essential nutrition to your body? If so, these Refreshing Smoothies are for you! They are easy and quick to make, and contain great quality ingredients that will leave you feeling revitalized. These smoothies are great to have for breakfast, after practicing yoga, before going on a stroll to the park, or even before heading out on a family road trip. Whatever your vitality needs, these smoothies will give you lots of great, fresh ideas to help your body regain its strength. You'll definitely like the energy and lightness you'll feel when incorporating these smoothies into your diet.

Almond Glee Smoothie

Crunchier than any other tree nut, almonds are fun to snack on and delicious to add to a smoothie! These little treats are perfect to nibble on throughout the day, but the unique taste they give smoothies is out of this world. If you're looking for a great source of the antioxidant vitamin E, just 1 ounce of almonds gives you more than a third of the Recommended Daily Value. Talk about being a health nut! *Note: Why should you soak the almonds overnight before adding to your smoothie? Soaked almonds can be easier to digest. It also makes it easier for your body to absorb the amount of nutrients and vitamins.*

Time: 5 minutes | **Difficulty:** Easy | **Yields:** 16 ounces | **Serving size:** 8 ounces

2 frozen bananas
⅓ cup almonds, soaked in water overnight
**   (drain water prior to adding)**
⅓ cup canned coconut milk
1 cup coconut water
2 tablespoons raw honey

Place all ingredients in blender and blend on high until smooth.

NUTRITIONAL INFORMATION (PER SERVING SIZE):

CALORIES:	CARBOHYDRATES:	PROTEIN:	FAT:	SODIUM:	FIBER:	SUGAR:
357.15 (kcal)	53 (g)	6.2 (g)	16 (g)	266 (mg)	13 (g)	70.5 (g)

Strawberry Blondie Smoothie

Say hello to one of the most delicious, juicy fruits around, the strawberry! When you eat a strawberry, you may focus solely on its taste, but this fruit is also a bona-fide superfood. Full of antioxidants and half of your daily value of vitamin C, just a ½ cup of strawberries can help you avoid wrinkles and boost your immune system. Other properties of strawberries have been shown to help eye health, suppress cancer cell growth, and more! Not only do they make your taste buds dance, they'll keep your body strong!

Time: 5 minutes | **Difficulty:** Easy | **Yields:** 16 ounces | **Serving size:** 8 ounces

1 cup frozen strawberries
1 frozen banana
⅓ cup walnuts
¼ teaspoon vanilla extract
2 tablespoons raw honey
1 cup unsweetened almond milk

Place all ingredients in blender and blend on high until smooth.

NUTRITIONAL INFORMATION (PER SERVING SIZE):

CALORIES:	CARBOHYDRATES:	PROTEIN:	FAT:	SODIUM:	FIBER:	SUGAR:
290 (kcal)	40.4 (g)	4.5 (g)	14 (g)	185.7 (mg)	9.7 (g)	57.5 (g)

Mango Delight Smoothie

What is round, orange, and prevents cancer, lowers cholesterol, clears the skin, promotes eye health, and helps diabetes? The mango! Who knew such a delicious fruit could be such a natural gift of health? Packed full of vitamin C, vitamin A, and carotenoids, these juicy delights will help keep your immune system running strong. Add them to your smoothie and show your delight inside and out!

Time: 5 minutes | **Difficulty:** Easy | **Yields:** 24 ounces | **Serving size:** 8 ounces

2½ cups frozen mango slices
½ cup canned coconut milk, chilled overnight
1½ cups coconut water
1 tablespoon raw honey
Juice of ½ lime
¼ teaspoon cinnamon

Place all ingredients in blender and blend on high until smooth.

NUTRITIONAL INFORMATION (PER SERVING SIZE):

CALORIES:	CARBOHYDRATES:	PROTEIN:	FAT:	SODIUM:	FIBER:	SUGAR:
210 (kcal)	34.96 (g)	2.6 (g)	8 (g)	78 (mg)	12.25 (g)	70.5 (g)

Sunshiny Day Smoothie

With tasty chunks of pineapple and banana, bright lemon juice, and more, this little concoction will make your taste buds sing with joy . . . and all of the health benefits that this smoothie provides will have your insides singing along. Packed with vitamin A, vitamin C, calcium, phosphorus, and potassium, the pineapple alone in this smoothie can help strengthen bones, prevent coughs and colds, and keep your gums healthy. Drink this little treat and rejoice!

Time: 5 minutes | **Difficulty:** Easy | **Yields:** 20 ounces | **Serving size:** 10 ounces

2 cups frozen pineapple chunks
1 frozen banana
1 cup kale
1 cup filtered water
Juice of ½ lemon
½ teaspoon freshly grated ginger

Place all ingredients in blender and blend on high until smooth.

NUTRITIONAL INFORMATION (PER SERVING SIZE):

CALORIES:	CARBOHYDRATES:	PROTEIN:	FAT:	SODIUM:	FIBER:	SUGAR:
154.5 (kcal)	40 (g)	2.5 (g)	0 (g)	34 (mg)	8 (g)	46.5 (g)

Funky Kiwi Smoothie

Want a sweet treat that is guilt free? Kiwi's low glycemic index will do just the trick. Compared with other foods, kiwis will not cause a strong insulin rush in your body, allowing you to enjoy exotic sweetness without storing any extra fat! Kiwis are a great source of fiber as well; they help support a healthy digestive tract and will reduce your chances of intestinal problems. Mixed with honeydew and mint leaves, this amazing Funky Kiwi Smoothie gives you the exotic freshness that your body craves.

Time: 5 minutes | **Difficulty:** Easy | **Yields:** 16 ounces | **Serving size:** 8 ounces

1 cup frozen strawberries
4 kiwis, skin removed
1 cup honeydew melon
Juice of ½ lemon
5 mint leaves
2 tablespoons raw honey

Place all ingredients in blender and blend on high until smooth.

NUTRITIONAL INFORMATION (PER SERVING SIZE):

CALORIES:	CARBOHYDRATES:	PROTEIN:	FAT:	SODIUM:	FIBER:	SUGAR:
214 (kcal)	53.5 (g)	3 (g)	0 (g)	43 (mg)	12 (g)	83.5 (g)

Grape Escape Smoothie

Grapes are not only sweet, juicy, and refreshing, they are a nice snack in between meals or when you are on the go! Add these little guys to your smoothies for a healthy sweetness that will do your body good. In addition to being delicious, due to their low glycemic index, grapes have been shown to support a better blood sugar balance while helping your body better regulate insulin. Low glycemic index foods help you keep your blood sugar balance under control in order to maintain, or help you lose, weight. Regulating insulin and keeping insulin sensitivity in control can help you avoid diabetes and improve your overall health. Sounds like a win-win!

Time: 5 minutes | **Difficulty:** Easy | **Yields:** 20 ounces | **Serving size:** 10 ounces

1 frozen banana
½ cup frozen blueberries
1 cup seedless purple grapes
1 cup baby kale
1 cup coconut water

Place all ingredients in blender and blend on high until smooth.

NUTRITIONAL INFORMATION (PER SERVING SIZE):

CALORIES:	CARBOHYDRATES:	PROTEIN:	FAT:	SODIUM:	FIBER:	SUGAR:
165 (kcal)	40.25 (g)	3.25 (g)	0 (g)	285.5 (mg)	10 (g)	50.5 (g)

Orchard Medley Smoothie

If you're looking for a Paleo smoothie that's as healthy as it is refreshing, the Orchard Medley Smoothie is right up your alley! Thanks to the pears in this recipe, this smoothie is packed with fiber. In fact, pears are one of the highest fiber fruits on the planet, offering 6 grams per medium-sized fruit! The recommended daily intake of fiber is 25–30 grams per day, so drinking just one serving of this smoothie a day will help you on your way to great health. Fiber helps lower cholesterol, is good for your digestive health, and can even help improve blood sugar levels as it slows the absorption of sugar. But fiber is only one of the things pears have to offer. They also contain a fair amount of vitamins K, C, B_2, B_3, and B_6 . . . not to mention the amazing taste they bring to a smoothie! Try having at least one pear a day, and enjoy a healthy and satisfying treat!

Time: 5 minutes | **Difficulty:** Easy | **Yields:** 20 ounces | **Serving size:** 10 ounces

2 ripe pears, cored
1 red apple, cored
1 cup seedless purple grapes
1 cup organic carrot juice
1 cup coconut water ice cubes

Place all ingredients in blender and blend on high until smooth.

NUTRITIONAL INFORMATION (PER SERVING SIZE):

CALORIES:	CARBOHYDRATES:	PROTEIN:	FAT:	SODIUM:	FIBER:	SUGAR:
223.5 (kcal)	58 (g)	2.5 (g)	0 (g)	74 (mg)	17 (g)	77 (g)

Honeybunches Smoothie

Looking for something sweet but don't want to pour a bunch of processed sugars into your smoothie? Raw honey will do just the trick. Not only is honey delicious, but studies have shown that honey actually has properties that can help your body better heal itself. Because of this, honey is actually being integrated into some modern medicines! In addition, honey can also help support higher energy levels, it contains good bacteria, and it can help slow aging. So you can have a sweet treat *and* be healthy? With the Honeybunches Smoothie, you sure can! *Note: Avoid feeding raw honey to children under the age of one; their digestive tracts are not quite ready to break down some aspects of this food.*

Time: 5 minutes | **Difficulty:** Easy | **Yields:** 20 ounces | **Serving size:** 10 ounces

1 cup frozen strawberries
1½ frozen bananas
1 cup baby spinach
1½ cups unsweetened almond milk
2 tablespoons raw honey
1 tablespoon sliced almonds (to garnish)

1. Place all ingredients in blender, except for the sliced almonds, and blend on high until smooth.
2. Pour smoothie in a glass and garnish with half of the sliced almonds. Enjoy!

NUTRITIONAL INFORMATION (PER SERVING SIZE):

CALORIES:	CARBOHYDRATES:	PROTEIN:	FAT:	SODIUM:	FIBER:	SUGAR:
200.75 (kcal)	65.5 (g)	3.25 (g)	2.25 (g)	301 (mg)	14.5 (g)	84 (g)

Orange You Glad It's Morning Smoothie

How can you not love oranges? They are so easy to eat for breakfast or a snack, and they give you a quick burst of energy to keep your day on track. These round little balls of goodness are also packed with nutrients and have a number of health benefits. With their citrus limonoids, chemical compounds found in citrus fruits, oranges can help fight forms of cancer including cancers of the skin, breast, lung, and colon. Oranges also can help prevent kidney disease, reduce the risk of liver cancer, lower cholesterol, boost heart heath, protect the skin, fight viral infections, and more! Orange you glad you're going to add them to your smoothie?

Time: 5 minutes | **Difficulty:** Easy | **Yields:** 20 ounces | **Serving size:** 10 ounces

1 frozen banana
1 cup frozen blackberries
1 seedless orange, peeled
1 cup baby spinach
½ cup canned coconut milk, chilled overnight
½ cup coconut water
1 tablespoon unsweetened shredded coconut (to garnish)

1. Place all ingredients in blender, except for the shredded coconut, and blend on high until smooth.
2. Pour smoothie in a glass and garnish with half of the shredded coconut. Enjoy!

NUTRITIONAL INFORMATION (PER SERVING SIZE):

CALORIES:	CARBOHYDRATES:	PROTEIN:	FAT:	SODIUM:	FIBER:	SUGAR:
248.75 (kcal)	31.4 (g)	4.4 (g)	14 (g)	60.7 (mg)	16.2 (g)	33.3 (g)

Healthy Cup Smoothie

This Paleo smoothie has all sorts of goodness packed into it, but one of the most important ingredients is the banana. The obvious benefit of adding a banana to a smoothie (or anything really) is its rich taste. Bananas taste great, but they also have a variety of health benefits. They contain high levels of tryptophan, an essential amino acid that helps create the happy-mood brain neurotransmitter serotonin. So be happy—and *feel* happy—with this delicious smoothie!

Time: 5 minutes | **Difficulty:** Easy | **Yields:** 20 ounces | **Serving size:** 10 ounces

1 frozen banana
1½ cups frozen blueberries
1 tablespoon cacao powder
1½ cups unsweetened almond milk
1 tablespoon raw honey
¼ cup mangos, diced (to garnish)
1 tablespoon unsweetened shredded coconut (to garnish)
1 tablespoon slivered almonds (to garnish)

1. Place all ingredients in blender, except for the garnish ingredients, and blend on high until smooth.
2. Pour smoothie in a glass and top with half of the mango, shredded coconut, and slivered almonds. Enjoy!

NUTRITIONAL INFORMATION (PER SERVING SIZE):

CALORIES:	CARBOHYDRATES:	PROTEIN:	FAT:	SODIUM:	FIBER:	SUGAR:
233.78 (kcal)	45.1 (g)	3.6 (g)	6 (g)	277.11 (mg)	14.85 (g)	60.56 (g)

Tropical Sway Smoothie

Do you ever daydream that you are in a tropical climate, sipping on a refreshing smoothie, and living the good life? Of course! The tangerine flavor in this smoothie is perfect if you want the taste of a quick escape to a tropical climate. Tangerines are fresh, juicy, and delicious, and like many other natural foods, they have a lot of health benefits to offer. Believe it or not, they actually have a higher amount of antioxidants than oranges. In addition, they're a rich source of vitamin C, which can help prevent neurodegenerative diseases, support wound healing, and more. So after you've made this smoothie, kick back, relax, put on some soothing music, and imagine you're on an island somewhere enjoying a completely natural and healthy treat.

Time: 5 minutes | **Difficulty:** Easy | **Yields:** 20 ounces | **Serving size:** 10 ounces

Juice of 1 tangerine
Juice of 1 grapefruit
½ cup frozen mango slices
½ cup frozen pineapple chunks
1 cup spinach
5 fresh mint leaves
1 cup coconut water

1. Place tangerines and grapefruits in a juicer and follow its instructions. Use the juice only and discard the pulp.
2. Place all ingredients in blender and blend on high until smooth.

NUTRITIONAL INFORMATION (PER SERVING SIZE):

CALORIES:	CARBOHYDRATES:	PROTEIN:	FAT:	SODIUM:	FIBER:	SUGAR:
148 (kcal)	35.25 (g)	2.75 (g)	0 (g)	281.5 (mg)	6.5 (g)	38 (g)

Wake Up to Watermelon Smoothie

What is green on the outside, pink on the inside, and is packed with vitamin C, vitamin A, potassium, and magnesium? You guessed it, watermelon! This summertime favorite is full of flavor and contains enough fruit juice to quench your dry summer thirst. Watermelon is actually more than 90 percent water! And, if you need to get in one-third of the recommended daily value of vitamins A and C, all you need to do is consume a 10-ounce wedge of this delicious fruit and you're good to go! Watermelon also contains essential amino acids that can help relax blood vessels and improve circulation; because of this, it can help soothe sore muscles. So quench your thirst with this nutrient-packed and refreshing Paleo smoothie!

Time: 5 minutes | **Difficulty:** Easy | **Yields:** 16 ounces | **Serving size:** 8 ounces

1 cup frozen strawberries
1½ cups chilled watermelon chunks
Juice of ½ lime
1 tablespoon raw honey
5 mint leaves

Place all ingredients in blender and blend on high until smooth.

NUTRITIONAL INFORMATION (PER SERVING SIZE):

CALORIES:	CARBOHYDRATES:	PROTEIN:	FAT:	SODIUM:	FIBER:	SUGAR:
93.75 (kcal)	23 (g)	1.25 (g)	0 (g)	6.5 (mg)	4.5 (g)	40 (g)

Papaya Harmony Smoothie

The papaya is an exotic fruit that contains multiple nutrients that benefit your health. This fruit also helps your digestive system and provides various medicinal properties. Papayas have a soft flesh, with plenty of fiber, which helps with healthy digestion. They also have very high levels of vitamin C (more than lemons and oranges), which helps boost the immune system, provides anti-inflammatory agents, and removes free radicals from your body. Papayas have other important vitamins and minerals, including vitamin A, essential B-complex vitamins, potassium, and calcium. Enjoy! *Note: Before consuming papaya, rinse it under cold water, cut it in half lengthwise, remove its seeds, carefully cut its skin, and cut the flesh into small squares. You can either consume it immediately or freeze for later use.*

Time: 5 minutes | **Difficulty:** Easy | **Yields:** 20 ounces | **Serving size:** 10 ounces

1 frozen banana
1 cup papaya chunks
½ cup coconut meat
1 tablespoon macadamia butter
¼ teaspoon vanilla extract
1 cup unsweetened coconut milk (from carton, not canned)
3 coconut water ice cubes
1 teaspoon unsweetened shredded coconut (to garnish)

1. Place all ingredients in blender, except for the shredded coconut, and blend on high until smooth.
2. Pour smoothie in a glass and garnish with half of the shredded coconut. Enjoy!

NUTRITIONAL INFORMATION (PER SERVING SIZE):

CALORIES:	CARBOHYDRATES:	PROTEIN:	FAT:	SODIUM:	FIBER:	SUGAR:
251.75 (kcal)	28.3 (g)	2.75 (g)	16 (g)	46.8 (mg)	13.85 (g)	29.65 (g)

Just Peachy Smoothie

What has 65 calories, 0 grams of fat, and is extremely sweet and nourishing? Answer: 1 medium-size peach! This fruit has a good amount of fiber, ten different vitamins, minerals, and various antioxidants. All of this goodness aids vision; keeps skin from wrinkling and free radicals from multiplying; improves memory; and helps prevent blood problems, heart disease, hypertension, cardiac arrhythmia, fatigue, anxiety, muscle weakness, and skin problems. Peaches are deliciously sweet and extremely refreshing, making them an ideal smoothie ingredient. Mixing the peaches, strawberries, honey, and other ingredients in this Just Peachy Smoothie will give you the kick-start you need in your day!

Time: 5 minutes | **Difficulty:** Easy | **Yields:** 20 ounces | **Serving size:** 10 ounces

2 cups frozen peach slices
1 cup frozen strawberries
1 cup spinach
1 tablespoon raw honey
1¼ cups coconut water

Place all ingredients in blender and blend on high until smooth.

NUTRITIONAL INFORMATION (PER SERVING SIZE):

CALORIES:	CARBOHYDRATES:	PROTEIN:	FAT:	SODIUM:	FIBER:	SUGAR:
148.75 (kcal)	35.13 (g)	3.25 (g)	0 (g)	342 (mg)	11.75 (g)	34 (g)

Pineapple Sunshine Smoothie

Pineapple is a native South American tropical fruit that offers various health benefits. It's a fantastic source of vitamins A and C, potassium, copper, and manganese. These vitamins and minerals—powerful antioxidants—help keep blood vessels, skin, organs, and bones healthy, and they help control blood pressure. Pineapple also helps fight indigestion and arthritis. It is also low in calories, which makes it an ideal fruit to add to your Paleo smoothies! *Note: When you're at the grocery store shopping for pineapple, be sure to buy the one that has the strongest and sweetest smell. This means that the fruit is perfectly ripened and extra sweet; when you get home, slice the pineapple right away (freeze it if not consumed immediately) and add it to your Paleo smoothie.*

Time: 5 minutes | **Difficulty:** Easy | **Yields:** 20 ounces | **Serving size:** 10 ounces

1 cup frozen pineapple chunks
1 frozen banana
1 cup ripe mango slices
1½ cups coconut water

Place all ingredients in blender and blend on high until smooth.

NUTRITIONAL INFORMATION (PER SERVING SIZE):

CALORIES:	CARBOHYDRATES:	PROTEIN:	FAT:	SODIUM:	FIBER:	SUGAR:
181.5 (kcal)	45.2 (g)	3 (g)	0 (g)	60 (mg)	12.5 (g)	63 (g)

Recovery Smoothies

Recovery means going back to your ideal condition, taking your body back to where you ultimately want to be. In today's world, you may not have control over the situations that surround you, and after long, taxing days, almost nothing sounds better than just taking time to unwind and recoup. Everyone has had a tough workday, an exhausting workout, or a difficult life situation. These types of situations drain your body of essential minerals, vitamins, and nutrients, but with the smoothies found in this section, you can soothe your body and treat it to something good! So take the time to give your body a Paleo smoothie that will get rid of that exhausted and overworked feeling and allow you to feel like new. Your body will thank you!

Power-Up Smoothie

You may not have thought to put an egg into a smoothie, but after you taste this Power-Up Smoothie, you'll be a convert! An egg won't affect the taste, and you will be getting more of the nutrients you need in a new delicious way. Eggs contain essential nutrients and have 2 antioxidants that contribute to eye health. Eggs are also high in protein—each egg contributes around 13 percent of your Recommended Daily Value—which is important for muscle recovery. Protein provides the body with what it needs to repair tissues. The high amount of protein in eggs also helps the body regulate weight loss if eaten with a healthy diet. So don't be afraid to try out this recipe. You'll be glad you did!

Time: 15 minutes | **Difficulty:** Medium | **Yields:** 20 ounces | **Serving size:** 10 ounces

2 eggs
1 frozen banana
1 cup frozen blueberries
1½ cups coconut water
1 cup firmly packed spinach
1 tablespoon coconut butter
1 tablespoon ground flaxseed
½ teaspoon ground cinnamon
½ teaspoon ground ginger

1. Place eggs in a small pot and fill with hot tap water. Heat uncovered pot over medium heat and bring water to a boil, about 2 minutes. Once water boils, set timer for 6 minutes, then remove eggs and let cool.
2. Once eggs have cooled, peel them, then add all ingredients to blender. Blend on high until smooth.

NUTRITIONAL INFORMATION (PER SERVING SIZE):

CALORIES:	CARBOHYDRATES:	PROTEIN:	FAT:	SODIUM:	FIBER:	SUGAR:
255.5 (kcal)	33.7 (g)	9.5 (g)	9 (g)	210 (mg)	15 (g)	39 (g)

PB and J Smoothie

Who doesn't love peanut butter and jelly? It's a popular combination that you may remember from your childhood. But wait a minute! Peanut butter is a no-no on the Paleo diet due to the processing required for peanuts. Fortunately, this Paleo PB and J Smoothie uses extremely tasty and healthy cashew butter! Cashews contain copper, manganese, tryptophan, magnesium, and phosphorus, minerals that create the happy-mood brain neurotransmitter serotonin and help with the development of bones and connective tissues. Cashews also have unsaturated fatty acids that promote cardiovascular health. So get nutty with these nuts and enjoy a classic PB and J-tasting smoothie!

Time: 5 minutes | **Difficulty:** Easy | **Yields:** 20 ounces | **Serving size:** 10 ounces

1 cup frozen strawberries
1 frozen banana
2 cups unsweetened almond milk
2 tablespoons cashew butter
2 Medjool dates, pitted
½ teaspoon cinnamon

Place all ingredients in blender and blend on high until smooth.

NUTRITIONAL INFORMATION (PER SERVING SIZE):

CALORIES:	CARBOHYDRATES:	PROTEIN:	FAT:	SODIUM:	FIBER:	SUGAR:
281.75 (kcal)	44.5 (g)	5.5 (g)	11.5 (g)	367.5 (mg)	12 (g)	54 (g)

Pearfect Smoothie

The combination of banana and pear with the added splash of pear juice makes this smoothie equal parts healthy and amazing. How could it not be with such wonderful ingredients? After all, pears are packed with fiber, and you know that bananas are pretty impressive too! Bananas can also help you avoid cramps, build strong bones, reduce digestive constipation, and help reduce heartburn. These are only a few ways you will benefit from bananas, and there are many more benefits too. So enjoy the subtle banana taste in this smoothie while reaping its health benefits!

Time: 5 minutes | **Difficulty:** Easy | **Yields:** 16 ounces | **Serving size:** 8 ounces

1 frozen banana
1 ripe pear, cored
1 cup seedless green grapes
1 teaspoon grapeseed oil
1 cup organic pear juice

Place all ingredients in blender and blend on high until smooth.

NUTRITIONAL INFORMATION (PER SERVING SIZE):

CALORIES:	CARBOHYDRATES:	PROTEIN:	FAT:	SODIUM:	FIBER:	SUGAR:
192.5 (kcal)	44.5 (g)	2 (g)	2.5 (g)	10 (mg)	9 (g)	72 (g)

Cashew Protein Smoothie

You'll notice that several recipes throughout this book contain cashews as a substitute for peanuts. As you know, peanuts are highly processed, and cashews are just as tasty and have amazing health benefits. Try drinking this Cashew Protein Smoothie regularly to help with weight loss. One 28-month study involving 8,865 adult men and women in Spain found that participants who ate nuts at least twice a week were 31 percent less likely to gain weight than participants who never or almost never ate nuts. What else helps fight weight gain? Protein! Protein is also important for muscle recovery and provides the body with what it needs to repair tissues. So cash in on the cashews, and enjoy this healthy recovery smoothie!

Time: 5 minutes | **Difficulty:** Easy | **Yields:** 20 ounces | **Serving size:** 10 ounces

1 cup frozen blueberries
1 frozen banana
½ avocado
1 cup spinach
1½ cups unsweetened coconut milk (from carton, not canned)
¼ cup cashews, soaked in water overnight
  (drain water before using)
2 fresh mint leaves
3 tablespoons unsweetened shredded coconut
1 tablespoon raw honey
¼ teaspoon cinnamon

Place all ingredients in blender and blend on high until smooth.

NUTRITIONAL INFORMATION (PER SERVING SIZE):

CALORIES:	CARBOHYDRATES:	PROTEIN:	FAT:	SODIUM:	FIBER:	SUGAR:
450 (kcal)	49.5 (g)	8 (g)	27.5 (g)	34 (mg)	20.25 (g)	53.5 (g)

Tropical Revival Smoothie

Close your eyes and visualize a tropical paradise where sweet mangos, pineapples, and bananas are plentiful. You can almost taste the sweet, satisfying flavors that quench your thirst and fill your belly with natural goodness. When you make this smoothie, you won't have to imagine it, you can experience it! This recipe includes all of these exotic fruits, and also adds in some baby spinach for good measure. Baby spinach brings its "A-game" when it comes to nutrient content. Low in calories and rich in vitamins K, A, C, and folate, the 2 cups of baby spinach in this recipe provides your body with 25 percent of the Recommended Daily Value for vitamin C, and nearly 400 percent for vitamin K. These nutrients help support blood health as well as bone health. Baby spinach, mixed with the other exotic nutrient-rich fruits, will make your taste buds dance with joy!

Time: 5 minutes | **Difficulty:** Easy | **Yields:** 20 ounces | **Serving size:** 10 ounces

1 frozen banana
½ cup frozen mango slices
½ cup frozen pineapple chunks 2 cups baby spinach
1½ cups unsweetened almond milk

Place all ingredients in blender and blend on high until smooth.

NUTRITIONAL INFORMATION (PER SERVING SIZE):

CALORIES:	CARBOHYDRATES:	PROTEIN:	FAT:	SODIUM:	FIBER:	SUGAR:
136.5 (kcal)	28.5 (g)	2.75 (g)	2.25 (g)	321.5 (mg)	9 (g)	34 (g)

Bananas for Coconut Smoothie

Looking for something that's good for your immune system? How about something that is also antiviral, antifungal, antibacterial, sweet, and all-around healthy? Meet the coconut! Coconuts have long been a food staple for many Pacific Islanders; many of whom even call the coconut tree the "Tree of Life." Coconuts contain a variety of vitamins, minerals, and amino acids, and are also a great source of fiber. They also have antioxidant properties, can be used to treat skin disorders, and support the development of strong bones and teeth. This Bananas for Coconut Smoothie combines coconut milk and shredded coconut, which adds just the right amount of flavor to this Paleo smoothie. Blend it up with a few other ingredients and see just what the Pacific Islanders have been raving about!

Time: 5 minutes | **Difficulty:** Easy | **Yields:** 16 ounces | **Serving size:** 8 ounces

**1 frozen banana
1 cup green apple, cored
1 cup baby spinach
½ cup canned coconut milk, chilled overnight
½ cup unsweetened coconut milk (from carton, not canned)
3 tablespoons unsweetened shredded coconut**

Place all ingredients in blender and blend on high until smooth.

NUTRITIONAL INFORMATION (PER SERVING SIZE):

CALORIES:	CARBOHYDRATES:	PROTEIN:	FAT:	SODIUM:	FIBER:	SUGAR:
267 (kcal)	28.5 (g)	2.75 (g)	18 (g)	53.5 (mg)	10.5 (g)	30.5 (g)

Cacao Recovery Smoothie

You may not have thought that cacao was a healthy option, but think again. Adding some cacao to your smoothie is not only allowed, it's encouraged! For many people any flavor of chocolate is a weakness, and cacao is the main ingredient used in the making of chocolate! As it turns out, cacao isn't such a bad thing; in fact, it's pretty amazing! This power food is full of minerals, antioxidants, and other nutrients that can stimulate your immune system, help oxygenate the brain, and even help you avoid heart disease. Mix this into your smoothie as a healthy way to add some delicious flavor. Enjoy!

Time: 5 minutes | **Difficulty:** Easy | **Yields:** 20 ounces | **Serving size:** 10 ounces

1½ cups frozen strawberries
1 frozen banana
1½ cups unsweetened almond milk
2 tablespoons almond butter
2 tablespoons raw honey
1 tablespoon cacao powder

Place all ingredients in blender and blend on high until smooth.

NUTRITIONAL INFORMATION (PER SERVING SIZE):

CALORIES:	CARBOHYDRATES:	PROTEIN:	FAT:	SODIUM:	FIBER:	SUGAR:
286.13 (kcal)	44.5 (g)	4.15 (g)	11.5 (g)	280.3 (mg)	11.7 (g)	59.5 (g)

Dates to the Rescue Smoothie

Although dates are high in sugar, they are a healthy alternative to artificial sweeteners, and actually boast some real health benefits. Dates are an excellent source of fiber; in fact, dates contain soluble fiber, which promotes healthy cholesterol and blood glucose levels in addition to helping with healthy digestion. These sweet treats also contain potassium, copper, and other essential nutrients that promote healthy blood pressure and overall blood cell health. Mix these with some other healthy fruits and you are in for one sweet and nutritious treat!

Time: 5 minutes | **Difficulty:** Easy | **Yields:** 20 ounces | **Serving size:** 10 ounces

2 frozen bananas
2 cups baby kale
1½ cups unsweetened vanilla almond milk
4 Medjool dates, pitted
¼ teaspoon cinnamon
1 teaspoon flaxseed meal

Place all ingredients in blender and blend on high until smooth.

NUTRITIONAL INFORMATION (PER SERVING SIZE):

CALORIES:	CARBOHYDRATES:	PROTEIN:	FAT:	SODIUM:	FIBER:	SUGAR:
313.4 (kcal)	72.9 (g)	4.75 (g)	2.6 (g)	331.7 (mg)	16.75 (g)	94 (g)

Feel Good Smoothie

Get a little healthy mix of everything with this Feel Good Smoothie! The amazing combination of bananas, spinach, almonds, and more is not only healthy, it's delicious too! You get the sweet and tropical flavors from the banana, coconut, honey, and almond combination, and a fabulous splash of nutrition from the spinach. This smoothie is meant to make you strong and give you lots of long-lasting energy. You will get a nice fix of "healthy" within a few sips. The mix of wonderful ingredients in this smoothie definitely do its name justice; how could you *not* feel good when drinking something this incredible?

Time: 5 minutes | **Difficulty:** Easy | **Yields:** 16 ounces | **Serving size:** 8 ounces

1 frozen banana
2 cups spinach
1¼ cups unsweetened almond milk
**½ cup almonds, soaked in water overnight
    (drain water before using)**
1 tablespoon unsweetened shredded coconut
2 tablespoons raw honey

Place all ingredients in blender and blend on high until smooth.

NUTRITIONAL INFORMATION (PER SERVING SIZE):

CALORIES:	CARBOHYDRATES:	PROTEIN:	FAT:	SODIUM:	FIBER:	SUGAR:
301.5 (kcal)	38.65 (g)	7.28 (g)	15.5 (g)	278.2 (mg)	12.95 (g)	51.3 (g)

Pumpkin Protein Smoothie

This smoothie is sure to be an autumn favorite; with pumpkin purée, pumpkin spice, and cinnamon, it really captures the taste of the season. The pumpkin purée is an excellent source of fiber. Fiber aids in digestion and helps your body absorb essential nutrients from the foods you are consuming. Pumpkin purée also contains a healthy dose of potassium, which also aids in digestion. (This might as well be called the digestion smoothie!) Another reason to add pumpkin purée to a smoothie is to support your immune system. Vitamin A and iron are found in pumpkin purée, and they help keep your eyes, bones, and teeth healthy. So enjoy this seasonal smoothie and keep your immune system in check, especially as the temperatures start to drop!

Time: 5 minutes | **Difficulty:** Easy | **Yields:** 16 ounces | **Serving size:** 8 ounces

2 frozen bananas
½ cup pumpkin purée
1 cup baby kale
1 cup unsweetened vanilla almond milk
1 tablespoon maple syrup
1 teaspoon cacao powder
¼ teaspoon cinnamon
¼ teaspoon pumpkin pie spice
1 teaspoon chia seeds

Place all ingredients in blender and blend on high until smooth.

NUTRITIONAL INFORMATION (PER SERVING SIZE):

CALORIES:	CARBOHYDRATES:	PROTEIN:	FAT:	SODIUM:	FIBER:	SUGAR:
204.53 (kcal)	45.13 (g)	3.85 (g)	2.75 (g)	220.55 (mg)	14.55 (g)	44 (g)

Fresh Fix Smoothie

Who can deny the crisp, delicious freshness of an apple? The skin, juice, and fruit are packed with flavor and nutrients. With an antioxidant concentration per serving size that is through the roof, these red gems are the perfect addition to any healthy creation, and smoothies are no exception. Bananas add even more health benefits to this amazing Paleo delight! This Fresh Fix Smoothie is sure to satisfy cravings and give your body the nourishment it deserves.

Time: 5 minutes | **Difficulty:** Easy | **Yields:** 20 ounces | **Serving size:** 10 ounces

1½ frozen bananas
1 red apple, cored
½ avocado
1 cup kale
1½ cups coconut water
2 Medjool dates, pitted

Place all ingredients in blender and blend on high until smooth.

NUTRITIONAL INFORMATION (PER SERVING SIZE):

CALORIES:	CARBOHYDRATES:	PROTEIN:	FAT:	SODIUM:	FIBER:	SUGAR:
318 (kcal)	83.95 (g)	5.5 (g)	7.5 (g)	95 (mg)	28.5 (g)	99.5 (g)

Cravings Crasher Smoothie

Craving something sweet, chocolaty, and a bit milky? This Cravings Crasher Smoothie is just what you need. Sometimes cravings can get the best of you, and tempt you to pick up the closest thing within reach. Don't do it! With the six healthy and natural ingredients found in this recipe, you get a little bit of everything, including healthy ingredients that don't sacrifice taste and are sure to curb the most incessant of cravings. With bananas, unsweetened almond milk, and cacao powder, you are getting loads of potassium, vitamin D, calcium, vitamin E, and more. Enjoy this treat before grabbing the bag of Oreos, and you'll be happy you did!

Time: 5 minutes | **Difficulty:** Easy | **Yields:** 20 ounces | **Serving size:** 10 ounces

2 frozen bananas
1½ cups unsweetened almond milk
¼ cup unsweetened shredded coconut
2 tablespoons almond butter
2 Medjool dates, pitted
1 tablespoon cacao powder

Place all ingredients in blender and blend on high until smooth.

NUTRITIONAL INFORMATION (PER SERVING SIZE):

CALORIES:	CARBOHYDRATES:	PROTEIN:	FAT:	SODIUM:	FIBER:	SUGAR:
377.25 (kcal)	54.1 (g)	5.35 (g)	18.5 (g)	284.3 (mg)	17.8 (g)	62.2 (g)

Cherry on Top Smoothie

Cherries aren't just for ice cream sundaes. These little balls of deliciousness add just the right touch when added to a smoothie—and they're good for you too! Cherries can help reduce the pain associated with arthritis and can even help fight cancer. Containing a large amount of flavonoids (antioxidants), cherries can help your body rid itself of harmful free radicals, and they're packed with potassium, which can lower your blood pressure. If you have a high-sodium diet, the potassium in cherries can help your body achieve a healthier balance. Lastly, cherries can support weight loss; their B vitamins are crucial for a healthy metabolism. Enjoy!

Time: 5 minutes | **Difficulty:** Easy | **Yields:** 20 ounces | **Serving size:** 10 ounces

1½ frozen bananas
¼ cup frozen sweet cherries, pitted
½ avocado
1 cup spinach
1 hard-boiled egg
1 cup coconut water

Place all ingredients in blender and blend on high until smooth.

NUTRITIONAL INFORMATION (PER SERVING SIZE):

CALORIES:	CARBOHYDRATES:	PROTEIN:	FAT:	SODIUM:	FIBER:	SUGAR:
235.13 (kcal)	53 (g)	7.13 (g)	10 (g)	348.5 (mg)	20.25 (g)	54 (g)

Get Up and Dance Smoothie

One of the best things in this world is your ability to get up and dance. But to dance you must have energy! Eating healthy and giving your body what it needs is one of the best ways to maintain healthy energy and live a vibrant life. Fortunately, this smoothie contains the chia seed, which will do just that! This little ingredient is rich in omega-3 fatty acids, has a high fiber content, and is high in antioxidants, minerals, and more. These small seeds also help regulate blood sugar, reducing insulin resistance and helping decrease the risk of diabetes. Add these to the other healthy ingredients in this smoothie, and get ready to get up and dance!

Time: 5 minutes | **Difficulty:** Easy | **Yields:** 16 ounces | **Serving size:** 8 ounces

2 frozen bananas
1¼ cups unsweetened almond milk
2 tablespoons cashew butter
2 Medjool dates, pitted
1 tablespoon chia seeds

Place all ingredients in blender and blend on high until smooth.

NUTRITIONAL INFORMATION (PER SERVING SIZE):

CALORIES:	CARBOHYDRATES:	PROTEIN:	FAT:	SODIUM:	FIBER:	SUGAR:
327.45 (kcal)	53.75 (g)	6.18 (g)	12 (g)	233.9 (mg)	16.15 (g)	61 (g)

Never Beet Smoothie

This delicious root contains antioxidants that can protect you against coronary artery disease and strokes. It also offers anti-aging effects and helps lower cholesterol levels. Even though beets are low-caloric foods, they are packed with fiber, vitamins, minerals, and antioxidants. They are a very rich source of glycine betaine, which helps lower homocysteine levels in the blood to keep it from clotting and developing problems such as coronary heart disease, stroke, and vascular diseases. Beets are fantastic to add to smoothies not only because of their amazing health benefits, but also because of the unique taste they give each drink. Enjoy!

Time: 15 minutes | **Difficulty:** Medium | **Yields:** 20 ounces | **Serving size:** 10 ounces

⅓ **cup cooked beets**
1 frozen banana
1 cup frozen mixed berries
1 cup baby spinach
1½ cups unsweetened almond milk
¼ **teaspoon vanilla extract**
1 teaspoon chia seeds

1. Bring a small pot of water to a boil. Boil beets for 5 minutes. Remove from heat, rinse with cold water, and let cool; remove skin.
2. Place all ingredients in blender and blend on high until smooth.

NUTRITIONAL INFORMATION (PER SERVING SIZE):

CALORIES:	CARBOHYDRATES:	PROTEIN:	FAT:	SODIUM:	FIBER:	SUGAR:
146.25 (kcal)	27.78 (g)	2.95 (g)	3.65 (g)	309.1 (mg)	17.6 (g)	29.05 (g)

Cleansing Smoothies

Think about all those times when you've dined at fast-food restaurants, or those times when you forgot to wash your strawberries or apples before eating them, or even those times when you've left a restaurant feeling uncomfortable, as if something you ate was just not right! Your body works hard for you on a daily basis, and with the smoothies in this section, it's time to repay your body for all it does. Fortunately, drinking these Paleo smoothies as meal substitutes allows for easy digestion, and is one of the best things you can do to reimburse your body for all it does for you. Drinking these nutrient-rich smoothies boosts the enzymes in your body that nourish important detoxifying organs like your kidneys, liver, and colon. In turn, your organs will function more effectively and efficiently, helping your body rid itself of toxins. Also, all the leafy greens added to some of these smoothies carry great amounts of chlorophyll, which help your body become more alkaline and can help prevent unwanted diseases from forming. So take care of your body; you only have one, and you want it to last a long, long time! With these Cleansing Smoothies, you can help ensure your body stays healthy for all those days that are still to come. Take charge and help yourself live well.

Rest and Digest Cherry Smoothie

Cherries are fantastic in Paleo smoothies because they provide a sweet taste and mix very well with other ingredients. They are also one of the few fruits that contain a hormone called melatonin. Melatonin calms you down and makes you sleepy, which is why this Rest and Digest Cherry Smoothie is a great recipe to try at night before bed. Cherries are low in calories but rich in various nutrients, vitamins, and minerals, including vitamin C, potassium, iron, zinc, copper, and manganese. This fruit also has important antioxidants, such as beta-carotene and lutein, which will protect your body from free radicals that cause rapid aging and cancer. Cherries are also anti-inflammatory and help reduce the risk of heart disease. What's not to love?

Time: 5 minutes | **Difficulty:** Easy | **Yields:** 20 ounces | **Serving size:** 10 ounces

1 cup frozen sweet cherries, pitted
1 frozen banana
2 cups firmly packed baby spinach
1½ cups unsweetened coconut milk (from carton, not canned)
2 tablespoons raw honey
¼ teaspoon almond extract

Place all ingredients in blender and blend on high until smooth.

NUTRITIONAL INFORMATION (PER SERVING SIZE):

CALORIES:	CARBOHYDRATES:	PROTEIN:	FAT:	SODIUM:	FIBER:	SUGAR:
215.5 (kcal)	48.5 (g)	2 (g)	3.25 (g)	73.5 (mg)	9.5 (g)	74.5 (g)

Blueberry Goodness Smoothie

Packed with antioxidants, blueberries are great for your health, and they're a delicious addition to any smoothie. In fact, they have more antioxidants than any other fresh fruit. Need to boost your immune system? These little guys can help do the trick. Another key ingredient in this smoothie is almond milk. Not only is it a healthy alternative to dairy, it can help with weight management, heart health, and more! So what are you waiting for? Whip up this Paleo smoothie and enjoy the sweet blueberry and almond milk goodness!

Time: 5 minutes | **Difficulty:** Easy | **Yields:** 16 ounces | **Serving size:** 8 ounces

1½ cups frozen blueberries
1½ cups unsweetened vanilla almond milk
2 Medjool dates, pitted
¼ teaspoon cinnamon
⅛ teaspoon nutmeg (to garnish)

1. Place all ingredients in blender, except for the nutmeg, and blend on high until smooth.
2. Pour smoothie in a glass and garnish with half of the nutmeg. Enjoy!

NUTRITIONAL INFORMATION (PER SERVING SIZE):

CALORIES:	CARBOHYDRATES:	PROTEIN:	FAT:	SODIUM:	FIBER:	SUGAR:
163.7 (kcal)	35.5 (g)	2 (g)	2.25 (g)	272 (mg)	11.25 (g)	56 (g)

Papaya Cheer Smoothie

When you close your eyes while drinking this smoothie you'll immediately recognize the sweet notes coming from the mangos, the vibrant tanginess coming from the pineapple, and the musky undertones coming from the papaya. You'll also notice a touch of spice from the ginger and the cloves, which adds a unique aromatic richness to the mix. Stay cheery with this blissful treat that will awaken your senses and take you directly to a tropical paradise.

Time: 5 minutes | **Difficulty:** Easy | **Yields:** 16 ounces | **Serving size:** 8 ounces

½ cup frozen pineapple chunks
½ cup frozen mango slices
½ cup papaya chunks
1 cup coconut water
1 tablespoon raw honey
⅛ teaspoon ground ginger
⅛ teaspoon ground cloves

Place all ingredients in blender and blend on high until smooth.

NUTRITIONAL INFORMATION (PER SERVING SIZE):

CALORIES:	CARBOHYDRATES:	PROTEIN:	FAT:	SODIUM:	FIBER:	SUGAR:
116.5 (kcal)	28.65 (g)	1.75 (g)	0 (g)	258.3 (mg)	7.1 (g)	47.5 (g)

Cranberry Superhero Smoothie

Superheroes are awesome, right? The very thought of being superhuman might get your imagination running wild. Well, most people aren't born with superpowers, but you can work with what you have . . . your body! Adding cranberries and other healthy ingredients to this Cranberry Superhero Smoothie will help keep your body nourished and can help optimize your health. Cranberries have vitamin C and fiber, and are low in calories. Believe it or not, these superhero fruits actually have more antioxidants than broccoli, cherries, and many other healthy foods. So grab a handful for a snack, add them to smoothies for flavor, and feel super!

Time: 5 minutes | **Difficulty:** Easy | **Yields:** 16 ounces | **Serving size:** 8 ounces

1½ frozen bananas
½ cup fresh cranberries, pitted
1 seedless orange, peeled
1 cup kale
1 cup coconut water
Juice of ½ lemon

Place all ingredients in blender and blend on high until smooth.

NUTRITIONAL INFORMATION (PER SERVING SIZE):

CALORIES:	CARBOHYDRATES:	PROTEIN:	FAT:	SODIUM:	FIBER:	SUGAR:
156.5 (kcal)	58.25 (g)	4 (g)	0 (g)	285 (mg)	17.5 (g)	59.5 (g)

Soothing Lavender Smoothie

Lavender buds? You may be wondering what these are or why you'd want to add them to a smoothie. They come from the lavender plant, and one of lavender's wonderful gifts is its ability to relieve anxiety and tension in a natural way. Life can get stressful, and it's important to unwind and stop to breathe once in a while. Lavender can help ease the tension of life's daily stresses. Add this special ingredient to your smoothies and enjoy a soothing and delicious treat.

Time: 5 minutes | **Difficulty:** Easy | **Yields:** 20 ounces | **Serving size:** 10 ounces

1 frozen banana
½ cup frozen blueberries
½ cup frozen strawberries
1 teaspoon dried lavender buds
1½ cups unsweetened vanilla almond milk
1 teaspoon chia seeds

Place all ingredients in blender and blend on high until smooth.

NUTRITIONAL INFORMATION (PER SERVING SIZE):

CALORIES:	CARBOHYDRATES:	PROTEIN:	FAT:	SODIUM:	FIBER:	SUGAR:
128.3 (kcal)	24.5 (g)	2.1 (g)	3 (g)	273.58 (mg)	9.8 (g)	25 (g)

Grapefully Wholesome Smoothie

There are many things in this world to be thankful for, and it's worth taking a moment to appreciate the things that you may take for granted. One important thing to not take for granted is health. Fortunately, this smoothie has nutrients your body will thank you for. Grapes, the main ingredient in this wholesome creation, are tremendously delicious and nutritious. They help power up weight loss, support increased blood flow, and can even help the brain. As you drink this Grapefully Wholesome Smoothie, be thankful for the many blessings in life. Your body will thank you in return.

Time: 5 minutes | **Difficulty:** Easy | **Yields:** 20 ounces | **Serving size:** 10 ounces

1 frozen banana
½ cup frozen seedless red grapes
½ cup frozen seedless black grapes
1½ cups unsweetened almond milk
1 tablespoon raw honey
1 teaspoon flaxseed meal

Place all ingredients in blender and blend on high until smooth.

NUTRITIONAL INFORMATION (PER SERVING SIZE):

CALORIES:	CARBOHYDRATES:	PROTEIN:	FAT:	SODIUM:	FIBER:	SUGAR:
172.65 (kcal)	37.15 (g)	1.75 (g)	2.6 (g)	275.7 (mg)	5.5 (g)	54.5 (g)

Razzmatazz Smoothie

You'll love the tart kick of raspberry that's found in this smoothie. Raspberries have a low calorie count and a high fiber content, and are an extremely healthy fruit that can help with weight loss. They also have high levels of antioxidants that can lower the risk of cancer and slow the aging process. In addition, the high potassium and copper content in this delicious fruit helps give your body the nutrition it needs to produce red blood cells; potassium and copper can also help maintain healthy blood pressure. Raspberries also add a nice pop of flavor to your smoothie. So feed your body with this delicious and healthy Razzmatazz Smoothie!

Time: 5 minutes | **Difficulty:** Easy | **Yields:** 20 ounces | **Serving size:** 10 ounces

½ **cup frozen raspberries**
1 **frozen banana**
½ **cup ripe strawberries**
1½ **cups unsweetened almond milk**
1 **tablespoon almond butter**
⅛ **teaspoon almond extract**

Place all ingredients in blender and blend on high until smooth.

NUTRITIONAL INFORMATION (PER SERVING SIZE):

CALORIES:	CARBOHYDRATES:	PROTEIN:	FAT:	SODIUM:	FIBER:	SUGAR:
161.25 (kcal)	23.25 (g)	2.75 (g)	7 (g)	274.5 (mg)	11 (g)	20 (g)

Sweet Tater Smoothie

Sweet potato as a Paleo smoothie ingredient? That's right! The sweet potato is an amazing food that—believe it or not—even works well in smoothies. It's a great way to add some natural sweetness to a meal, smoothie, or snack. Sweet potatoes are packed full of vitamins B_6, C, D, and more that help protect your body against cold and flu viruses, help support healthy bones, help your body produce blood cells, and help accelerate wound healing. Sweet potatoes also contain iron and magnesium, minerals that help protect the body against stress. Enjoy this healthy and unique combination of ingredients to cleanse and fuel your body.

Time: 5 minutes | **Difficulty:** Easy | **Yields:** 16 ounces | **Serving size:** 8 ounces

1 frozen banana
1 baked medium sweet potato, skin removed
1¼ cups unsweetened vanilla almond milk
1 tablespoon maple syrup
¼ teaspoon cinnamon
¼ teaspoon nutmeg
⅛ teaspoon ground cloves (to garnish)

1. Place all ingredients in blender, except for the ground cloves, and blend on high until smooth.
2. Pour smoothie in a glass and garnish with half of the ground cloves. Enjoy!

NUTRITIONAL INFORMATION (PER SERVING SIZE):

CALORIES:	CARBOHYDRATES:	PROTEIN:	FAT:	SODIUM:	FIBER:	SUGAR:
157.5 (kcal)	33.55 (g)	2.13 (g)	1.9 (g)	269.6 (mg)	8.6 (g)	33 (g)

Strawberry Rhubarb Smoothie

Just hearing someone say "strawberry rhubarb" can make your mouth water! This Strawberry Rhubarb Smoothie will make your taste buds sing and give your body some much-needed vitamins and minerals at the same time. Rhubarb contains antioxidants, including lycopene and anthocyanins, which have been known to help fight disease. It also contains a healthy amount of vitamin K, which helps your body clot blood when needed and protect the bones. Rhubarb can also help fight cancers of the liver and prostate. With this summery Paleo smoothie, you'll get a fruity mix of deliciousness and help calm those not-so-healthy food cravings.

Time: 5 minutes | **Difficulty:** Easy | **Yields:** 20 ounces | **Serving size:** 10 ounces

1 cup frozen strawberries
1 cup frozen rhubarb chunks
½ frozen banana
1¼ cups unsweetened almond milk
1 tablespoon almond butter
1 tablespoon raw honey
1 teaspoon flaxseed meal

Place all ingredients in blender and blend on high until smooth.

NUTRITIONAL INFORMATION (PER SERVING SIZE):

CALORIES:	CARBOHYDRATES:	PROTEIN:	FAT:	SODIUM:	FIBER:	SUGAR:
179.15 (kcal)	26.65 (g)	2.88 (g)	6.5 (g)	236.2 (mg)	8.75 (g)	32.5 (g)

Coco-Nut Smoothie

Are you a nut for the coconut? With a creamy consistency and delicious taste, coconut milk is fantastic to add to a smoothie. In addition to being delicious, this amazing liquid is also full of vitamins C, E, B_1, B_3, B_5, and B_6; iron; calcium; and many other minerals that help keep your body healthy and repair damage your body and muscle tissues can incur over time. Want something to help calm your nerves *and* help you maintain healthy blood pressure? Coconut milk can help with that as well. Add this special ingredient to this Paleo smoothie and enjoy its taste and wonderful health benefits.

Time: 5 minutes | **Difficulty:** Easy | **Yields:** 20 ounces | **Serving size:** 10 ounces

1 cup frozen peach slices
½ cup frozen blueberries
1 ripe banana
1 cup baby kale
1¼ cups unsweetened coconut milk (from carton, not canned)
1 tablespoon minced walnuts

Place all ingredients in blender and blend on high until smooth.

NUTRITIONAL INFORMATION (PER SERVING SIZE):

CALORIES:	CARBOHYDRATES:	PROTEIN:	FAT:	SODIUM:	FIBER:	SUGAR:
172.03 (kcal)	31.5 (g)	2.8 (g)	5.5 (g)	61.85 (mg)	9.75 (g)	23.95 (g)

Blue-Pom Smoothie

Recently, it seems there have been a lot of pomegranate-based drinks and foods popping up, and for good reason. This fruit has a great taste and health benefits to boot. Punicalagins, compounds found in the pomegranate, are shown to benefit the heart and blood vessels, and not just in a small way. Studies have recently proven the major positive effect pomegranate juice has on reducing blood pressure. This delicious fruit is also full of antioxidants that will help keep you looking and feeling younger. So add pomegranate juice to this Paleo smoothie and enjoy great taste while keeping your body healthy.

Time: 5 minutes | **Difficulty:** Easy | **Yields:** 20 ounces | **Serving size:** 10 ounces

1 cup frozen blueberries
½ cup frozen blackberries
½ cup spinach
1¼ cups organic pomegranate juice
¼ cup canned coconut milk, chilled overnight
1 tablespoon raw honey
1 tablespoon pomegranate seeds (to garnish)

1. Place all ingredients in blender, except for the pomegranate seeds, and blend on high until smooth.
2. Pour smoothie in a glass and garnish with half of the pomegranate seeds. Enjoy!

NUTRITIONAL INFORMATION (PER SERVING SIZE):

CALORIES:	CARBOHYDRATES:	PROTEIN:	FAT:	SODIUM:	FIBER:	SUGAR:
234.48 (kcal)	46.1 (g)	1.88 (g)	7 (g)	51.6 (mg)	8.8 (g)	77.3 (g)

Sweet Kiwi Smoothie

The kiwi is a special ingredient in this Paleo smoothie. Kiwis have been shown to protect your body against macular degeneration and other eye problems, but that's not all! These little treats also help your body maintain an alkaline balance, which can result in deeper sleep, more youthful skin, and more. Combining kiwis and the other healthy fruits in this smoothie recipe will leave you feeling healthier without sacrificing any flavor.

Time: 5 minutes | **Difficulty:** Easy | **Yields:** 16 ounces | **Serving size:** 8 ounces

1 frozen banana
2 kiwis, skin removed
1 cup seedless green grapes
1 cup baby kale
1 cup unsweetened almond milk
1 tablespoon raw honey

Place all ingredients in blender and blend on high until smooth.

NUTRITIONAL INFORMATION (PER SERVING SIZE):

CALORIES:	CARBOHYDRATES:	PROTEIN:	FAT:	SODIUM:	FIBER:	SUGAR:
219 (kcal)	50.5 (g)	3.5 (g)	1.5 (g)	218 (mg)	10 (g)	68 (g)

Pink Grapefruit Smoothie

Like other citrus fruits, the grapefruit is full of vitamin C and other nutrients that your body craves. It can help with weight loss, too! The grapefruit is high in enzymes that help your body burn through fat and increase the body's metabolism. Grapefruits also contain lycopene, which helps reduce cancer-causing free radicals in the body. Amidst all of these nutrients, the grapefruit can also add some fresh flavor to your smoothie, especially when mixed with sweeter fruits like bananas and strawberries. So go out there and get the vitamins and minerals you need with this refreshing Pink Grapefruit Smoothie!

Time: 5 minutes | **Difficulty:** Easy | **Yields:** 16 ounces | **Serving size:** 8 ounces

1 frozen banana
1 cup frozen strawberries
1¼ cups ruby red grapefruit juice, preferably freshly squeezed
¼ cup canned coconut milk, chilled overnight
2 tablespoons raw honey
¼ teaspoon vanilla extract

Place all ingredients in blender and blend on high until smooth.

NUTRITIONAL INFORMATION (PER SERVING SIZE):

CALORIES:	CARBOHYDRATES:	PROTEIN:	FAT:	SODIUM:	FIBER:	SUGAR:
258.13 (kcal)	51.88 (g)	2.25 (g)	6 (g)	15 (mg)	6 (g)	56.5 (g)

Apple a Day Smoothie

We've all heard it, "an apple a day keeps the doctor away." Well, there is a reason that saying is still around. Apples have a laundry list of healthy benefits: They help maintain whiter and healthier teeth, protect against Parkinson's disease, help prevent cancer, decrease the risk of diabetes, and even support a healthier heart. This is only a small number of benefits that come with the delicious taste of the apple. Mix in some blueberries, and even more health benefits are in store for you. An Apple a Day Smoothie can help keep a lot more than just the doctor away!

Time: 5 minutes | **Difficulty:** Easy | **Yields:** 20 ounces | **Serving size:** 10 ounces

2 cups frozen blueberries
2 red apples, cored
1 cup unsweetened vanilla almond milk
½ cup coconut water
2 tablespoons raw honey

Place all ingredients in blender and blend on high until smooth.

NUTRITIONAL INFORMATION (PER SERVING SIZE):

CALORIES:	CARBOHYDRATES:	PROTEIN:	FAT:	SODIUM:	FIBER:	SUGAR:
256.5 (kcal)	62.25 (g)	2 (g)	1.5 (g)	204 (mg)	18.5 (g)	98 (g)

Plum Time Smoothie

This Plum Time Smoothie is just plum good. With a mix of banana, plums, almond milk, dates, and more, you get to taste a little bit of everything. Plums are full of potassium, a mineral that reduces blood pressure and can help reduce the risk of stroke. Plums are also full of antioxidants that can help keep free radicals under control, possibly reducing the risk of cancer and protecting your memory. Want to keep your digestive tract healthy? Plums can also help with this because they contain a good amount of fiber. What time is it? Plum smoothie time! Drink up!

Time: 5 minutes | **Difficulty:** Easy | **Yields:** 20 ounces | **Serving size:** 10 ounces

1 frozen banana
4 plums, cored
1 cup spinach
1½ cups unsweetened vanilla almond milk
3 Medjool dates, pitted
¼ teaspoon cinnamon

Place all ingredients in blender and blend on high until smooth.

NUTRITIONAL INFORMATION (PER SERVING SIZE):

CALORIES:	CARBOHYDRATES:	PROTEIN:	FAT:	SODIUM:	FIBER:	SUGAR:
250.5 (kcal)	59.5 (g)	2.5 (g)	2.75 (g)	295.75 (mg)	15 (g)	91.5 (g)

Dessert Smoothies

This smoothie section is a favorite. After all, who doesn't like sweets once in a while? It's important to indulge here and there, but indulging can mean different things to different people. Some people indulge with dark chocolate, some with heaping spoons of peanut butter, some with a juicy fruit, some with cappuccinos or large ice cream bowls. The smoothies in this section revolutionize indulging by teaching you how to let loose the Paleo-Smoothie way! There are recipes to satisfy your sweet tooth, no matter what you're craving. If you're looking for chocolate, try the Velvety Cacao Smoothie! If you're craving an apple pie, try the Sweet Apple Pie Smoothie. If you're dreaming about cheesecake, the Cheesecake Lover Smoothie will be perfect! No matter what you crave, you'll find a nice variety of Paleo dessert smoothies here. Give these recipes a try; you'll fall in love!

Sunflower Chocolate Smoothie

Sunflower seed butter is a fabulous substitute for any butter spread, as it's nut free, peanut free, and gluten free, making it a great solution for those on the Paleo diet who want to have a nut-free creamy spread and for those with allergies to such ingredients. Sunflower seed butter is a great nutritional source of fiber, zinc, iron, magnesium, and vitamin E, all of which help lower blood pressure and protect your body against damaging free radicals that cause chronic diseases. Ninety percent of the fats found in sunflower seed butter are unsaturated fats, which are healthy fats that help lower cholesterol and help fight against inflammation. Sunflower seed butter gives a creamy consistency to smoothies, making them so rich that it'll feel as if you're drinking a milkshake. This chocolate dream smoothie is a must-try!

Time: 5 minutes | **Difficulty:** Easy | **Yields:** 16 ounces | **Serving size:** 8 ounces

2 frozen bananas
1 teaspoon cacao powder
1½ cups unsweetened almond milk
4 Medjool dates, pitted
2 tablespoons organic unsweetened sunflower seed butter

Place all ingredients in blender and blend on high until smooth.

NUTRITIONAL INFORMATION (PER SERVING SIZE):

CALORIES:	CARBOHYDRATES:	PROTEIN:	FAT:	SODIUM:	FIBER:	SUGAR:
369.5 (kcal)	70 (g)	6.25 (g)	13 (g)	274 (mg)	18.5 (g)	95 (g)

Velvety Cacao Smoothie

What do you get when you mix a little cacao powder and banana? This delicious Velvety Cacao Smoothie, which is sure to satisfy you and remind you of the classic chocolate-dipped banana. But this recipe doesn't add additional sugars that are harmful to your body; instead, you get the sweet taste with added nutrients as well. Cacao powder is not only delicious, it can help improve heart function and alleviate stress as well. It contains vitamins B_1, B_2, B_3, B_5, B_9, and E, as well as minerals like magnesium, calcium, zinc, iron, and copper. By mixing this ingredient into your Paleo smoothie, you're guaranteed to nourish your body and satisfy your sweet tooth at the same time.

Time: 5 minutes | **Difficulty:** Easy | **Yields:** 16 ounces | **Serving size:** 8 ounces

1½ frozen bananas
1 teaspoon cacao powder
2 tablespoons cacao nibs
½ avocado
1½ cups unsweetened coconut milk (from carton, not canned)
2 tablespoons raw honey

Place all ingredients in blender and blend on high until smooth.

NUTRITIONAL INFORMATION (PER SERVING SIZE):

CALORIES:	CARBOHYDRATES:	PROTEIN:	FAT:	SODIUM:	FIBER:	SUGAR:
303 (kcal)	67.3 (g)	4.8 (g)	15 (g)	35.5 (mg)	24 (g)	79 (g)

Vanilla Shake Smoothie

You'll want to drink this amazing Vanilla Shake Smoothie after every meal once you taste the deliciousness of the vanilla bean! Vanilla is a delightful flavor that has worldwide popularity—and some even believe it to be a sexual stimulant. However, it has been proven that vanilla contains high levels of antioxidants that help the body fight off cancer-causing free radicals. Be sure to add the vanilla beans to this smoothie for a subtle but deliciously healthy-tasting Paleo drink.

Time: 5 minutes | **Difficulty:** Easy | **Yields:** 16 ounces | **Serving size:** 8 ounces

2 frozen bananas
1½ cups unsweetened almond milk
½ teaspoon fresh vanilla beans
1 tablespoon maple syrup
1 teaspoon unsweetened shredded coconut (to garnish)

1. Place all ingredients in blender, except for the shredded coconut, and blend on high until smooth.
2. Pour smoothie in a glass and garnish with half of the shredded coconut. Enjoy!

NUTRITIONAL INFORMATION (PER SERVING SIZE):

CALORIES:	CARBOHYDRATES:	PROTEIN:	FAT:	SODIUM:	FIBER:	SUGAR:
176.2 (kcal)	35.6 (g)	1.8 (g)	3.1 (g)	275.25 (mg)	7.85 (g)	40.15 (g)

Mint Chocolate Chip Smoothie

If mint chocolate chip is one of your favorite flavor combinations, you will love this Paleo concoction. Typically, mint chocolate chip anything is just loaded with dairy, which can not only be bad for your blood sugar, but is also one of the most inflammatory foods around today! Fortunately, this smoothie combines natural mint and chocolate in a healthy way. Mint has unique properties that are refreshing to smell and taste. It can help soothe the digestive tract, help rid the body of toxins, and can even reduce bad breath. Mix up this delicious Mint Chocolate Chip Smoothie and enjoy a healthy and guilt-free substitute to ice cream and other unhealthy treats.

Time: 5 minutes | **Difficulty:** Easy | **Yields:** 12 ounces | **Serving size:** 12 ounces

1 frozen banana
1 teaspoon cacao powder
1 tablespoon unsweetened carob chips
¼ teaspoon mint extract
½ cup canned coconut milk, chilled overnight
½ cup unsweetened coconut milk (from carton, not canned)

Place all ingredients in blender and blend on high until smooth.

NUTRITIONAL INFORMATION (PER SERVING SIZE):

CALORIES:	CARBOHYDRATES:	PROTEIN:	FAT:	SODIUM:	FIBER:	SUGAR:
391 (kcal)	36.5 (g)	5 (g)	29 (g)	49 (mg)	5.5 (g)	18 (g)

Sweet Apple Pie Smoothie

You've probably realized that apple pie isn't the healthiest treat in the world, so why not mix up an alternative in the form of a smoothie? The mix of apples, raw honey, and cinnamon is a perfect combination of flavor and nutrients. You know that apples are wholesome fruits, and when you add the honey and cinnamon, you throw a whole bunch of other healthy nutrients into the mix! Honey is loaded with essential vitamins and minerals including vitamins B_1, B_2, B_3, B_5, and B_6, as well as vitamin C. In fact, studies have shown that honey actually has properties that can help your body better heal itself. Just like honey, cinnamon packs a nice nutritional punch; recent research has shown that this delightful spice helps stabilize your blood sugar by increasing your glucose metabolism and improving your sensitivity to insulin. Cinnamon is amazing, isn't it? So next time you are craving some apple pie, mix up this delicious Paleo creation instead!

Time: 5 minutes | **Difficulty:** Easy | **Yields:** 16 ounces | **Serving size:** 8 ounces

2 apples, cored
1½ cups unsweetened vanilla almond milk
2 tablespoons raw honey
1 tablespoon organic unsweetened sunflower seed butter
¼ teaspoon cinnamon
¼ teaspoon nutmeg
¼ teaspoon apple pie spice
3 ice cubes

Place all ingredients in blender and blend on high until smooth.

NUTRITIONAL INFORMATION (PER SERVING SIZE):

CALORIES:	CARBOHYDRATES:	PROTEIN:	FAT:	SODIUM:	FIBER:	SUGAR:
228.15 (kcal)	41 (g)	2.25 (g)	7.5 (g)	289 (mg)	10.75 (g)	65.5 (g)

Berry Cacao Fantasy Smoothie

Raspberry, banana, and cacao, oh my! This smoothie is sure to be a favorite with its mix of sweet fruit, creamy almond milk, and a touch of cacao powder. All of the natural ingredients in this smoothie blend into a healthy and delicious creation. Packed with antioxidants and vitamin B$_6$, this Berry Cacao Fantasy Smoothie can help reduce the risk of dangerous and havoc-wreaking free radicals in the body, protect against muscle cramps, and reduce swelling. This delicious Paleo smoothie is packed full of flavor, vitamins, and minerals to keep your body running in tiptop shape!

Time: 5 minutes | **Difficulty:** Easy | **Yields:** 24 ounces | **Serving size:** 8 ounces

1 frozen banana
1 cup frozen raspberries
2 cups unsweetened vanilla almond milk
1 tablespoon cacao powder
2 tablespoons cashew butter
2 tablespoons raw honey

Place all ingredients in blender and blend on high until smooth.

NUTRITIONAL INFORMATION (PER SERVING SIZE):

CALORIES:	CARBOHYDRATES:	PROTEIN:	FAT:	SODIUM:	FIBER:	SUGAR:
192.3 (kcal)	30.3 (g)	3.7 (g)	8.3 (g)	369 (mg)	15 (g)	54 (g)

Sweet Orange Smoothie

The orange and chocolate flavor combination in this smoothie is enticing, intriguing, satisfying, and captivating. The tanginess of the orange mixes extremely well with the tartness of the chocolate, creating an indulgent fusion of seductive flavors. The sweet citrus taste of the oranges not only awakens your taste buds, it also quenches your thirst. So mix this smoothie up for breakfast, lunch, dinner, dessert, or a simple snack, and make life a little sweeter with this Sweet Orange Smoothie.

Time: 5 minutes | **Difficulty:** Easy | **Yields:** 16 ounces | **Serving size:** 8 ounces

1½ frozen bananas
1 seedless orange, peeled
1 teaspoon orange peel, grated
1 teaspoon cacao powder
1 tablespoon cacao nibs
1 cup unsweetened coconut milk (from carton, not canned)
1 tablespoon maple syrup
¼ teaspoon vanilla extract

Place all ingredients in blender and blend on high until smooth.

NUTRITIONAL INFORMATION (PER SERVING SIZE):

CALORIES:	CARBOHYDRATES:	PROTEIN:	FAT:	SODIUM:	FIBER:	SUGAR:
176.75 (kcal)	56.15 (g)	2.9 (g)	4.5 (g)	20.5 (mg)	16 (g)	64.5 (g)

Cheesecake Lover Smoothie

Do you have a weakness for cheesecake? Don't feel bad, it happens to the best of us. Although this smoothie doesn't completely substitute the texture and taste of traditional cheesecake, it still delivers delicious flavor and much more nutrition. Strawberries, almond milk, and more definitely make this smoothie a treat to behold. So next time you have the craving for some cheesecake, try a Cheesecake Lover Smoothie instead and get the nutrition and taste, without all the guilt!

Time: 5 minutes | **Difficulty:** Easy | **Yields:** 16 ounces | **Serving size:** 8 ounces

1 cup frozen strawberries
1½ cups unsweetened almond milk
½ cup cashews, soaked in water overnight (drain water before using)
2 Medjool dates, pitted
¼ teaspoon vanilla extract
1 teaspoon maple syrup
1 teaspoon coconut butter
1 teaspoon freshly squeezed lemon juice
1 teaspoon almond flour (to garnish)

1. Place all ingredients in blender, except for the almond flour, and blend on high until smooth.
2. Pour smoothie in a glass and garnish with half of the almond flour. Enjoy!

NUTRITIONAL INFORMATION (PER SERVING SIZE):

CALORIES:	CARBOHYDRATES:	PROTEIN:	FAT:	SODIUM:	FIBER:	SUGAR:
476.15 (kcal)	49.25 (g)	12.5 (g)	28.5 (g)	287.5 (mg)	13.5 (g)	55.4 (g)

Vanilla Coconut Cream Smoothie

One of the most amazing tastes in this world is coconut! It is sweet and likely reminds you of tropical climates. You can't help but imagine being on a sunny beach when you smell or taste coconut! Most people don't get to live on a sunny beach, so with this little drink you can just use your imagination. One thing you don't have to imagine, however, is the delicious taste. Let your mind wander to that beautiful sunny beach as you drink your fresh and healthy Vanilla Coconut Cream Smoothie.

Time: 5 minutes | **Difficulty:** Easy | **Yields:** 16 ounces | **Serving size:** 8 ounces

½ cup canned coconut milk, chilled overnight
1 cup unsweetened coconut milk (from carton, not canned)
3 Medjool dates, pitted
⅛ teaspoon vanilla bean seeds
¼ teaspoon vanilla extract
3 tablespoons unsweetened shredded coconut
1 tablespoon coconut butter
5 ice cubes

Place all ingredients in blender and blend on high until smooth. Enjoy!

NUTRITIONAL INFORMATION (PER SERVING SIZE):

CALORIES:	CARBOHYDRATES:	PROTEIN:	FAT:	SODIUM:	FIBER:	SUGAR:
329.4 (kcal)	34 (g)	3 (g)	23 (g)	39.75 (mg)	10.25 (g)	53 (g)

PearTastic Smoothie

Pears really are fantastic. They're crisp, delicious, and make for an excellent Paleo smoothie ingredient, as their flavor is easy to match and it blends smoothly. When you mix pears with Medjool dates, bananas, coconut milk, and sweet spices you'll experience an out-of-this world Paleo smoothie combination that will really brighten up your day! This particular smoothie is ideal for those afternoons where you need both a pick-me-up and a healthy, yet delicious, treat to satiate your cravings. The PearTastic Smoothie will give you lots of great energy and a nice array of antioxidants to keep your body healthy.

Time: 5 minutes | **Difficulty:** Easy | **Yields:** 16 ounces | **Serving size:** 8 ounces

1½ frozen bananas
2 ripe pears, cored
1 cup unsweetened coconut milk (from carton, not canned)
2 Medjool dates, pitted
1 teaspoon coconut cream concentrate
⅛ teaspoon nutmeg
⅛ teaspoon ground ginger
⅛ teaspoon cinnamon (to garnish)

1. Place all ingredients in blender, except for the cinnamon, and blend on high until smooth.
2. Pour smoothie in a glass and top smoothie with half of the cinnamon. Enjoy!

NUTRITIONAL INFORMATION (PER SERVING SIZE):

CALORIES:	CARBOHYDRATES:	PROTEIN:	FAT:	SODIUM:	FIBER:	SUGAR:
237.08 (kcal)	83.6 (g)	4.5 (g)	3.75 (g)	22.7 (mg)	23.5 (g)	107 (g)

CARIBBEAN SUNSET SMOOTHIE

BLUEBERRY GOODNESS SMOOTHIE

AÇAÍ BOOST SMOOTHIE

IT'S ALL YELLOW SMOOTHIE

SUNFLOWER CHOCOLATE SMOOTHIE

BERRY BOMB SMOOTHIE

NEVER BEET SMOOTHIE

COOL NECTARINE SMOOTHIE

MELON MANIA SMOOTHIE

GREEN FRUIT SMOOTHIE

PARADISE BEACH SMOOTHIE

PASSIONATE RASPBERRY SMOOTHIE

PAPAYA CHEER SMOOTHIE

PB AND J SMOOTHIE

PEARFECT SMOOTHIE

PAPAYA WAVE SMOOTHIE

PERFECT THREE SMOOTHIE

PINK SUMMER SMOOTHIE

PIÑA COLADA SMOOTHIE

PUMPKIN PIE SMOOTHIE

RAZZMATAZZ SMOOTHIE

TROPICAL GRAPE SMOOTHIE

SWEET TATER SMOOTHIE

STRAWBERRY MINT SMOOTHIE

VANILLA SHAKE SMOOTHIE

WAKE UP TO WATERMELON SMOOTHIE

Pumpkin Pie Smoothie

Pumpkin pie is definitely a seasonal favorite in many homes. The only problem with traditional pumpkin pie is that it tends to have a high amount of added sugar and fats. This smoothie recipe sticks with natural sweeteners like maple syrup and fruits to keep things clean and give your body what it craves without sacrificing taste. So instead of reaching for the pumpkin pie and putting on the seasonal pounds, mix up this alternative treat and feed your body the healthy way!

Time: 5 minutes | **Difficulty:** Easy | **Yields:** 16 ounces | **Serving size:** 8 ounces

1½ frozen bananas
½ cup pumpkin purée
1½ cups unsweetened almond milk
1 teaspoon maple syrup
¼ teaspoon vanilla extract
⅛ teaspoon ginger
⅛ teaspoon nutmeg
⅛ teaspoon allspice
⅛ teaspoon cinnamon (plus ⅛ teaspoon to garnish)

1. Place all ingredients in blender, except for the reserved cinnamon garnish, and blend on high until smooth.
2. Pour smoothie in a glass and garnish with half of the reserved cinnamon. Enjoy!

NUTRITIONAL INFORMATION (PER SERVING SIZE):

CALORIES:	CARBOHYDRATES:	PROTEIN:	FAT:	SODIUM:	FIBER:	SUGAR:
146.08 (kcal)	50.85 (g)	3 (g)	2.5 (g)	280.2 (mg)	14.25 (g)	52.5 (g)

Carrot Cake Smoothie

Who doesn't love carrots? They are crunchy, a little bit sweet, and you probably already know how healthy they are. A common problem with carrots, however, is that their health benefits are disguised when they're added to non-Paleo-approved dishes like carrot cakes and other desserts that contain highly processed ingredients and a large amount of sugar. Fortunately, this Carrot Cake Smoothie mimics the taste of a carrot cake and maintains the health factor of carrots without all the added junk, keeping it 100 percent Paleo. When added to the other healthy ingredients in this smoothie, this healthy and tasty smoothie is just waiting for you to sit down and enjoy!

Time: 5 minutes | **Difficulty:** Easy | **Yields:** 16 ounces | **Serving size:** 8 ounces

1½ frozen bananas
½ cup peeled and grated carrots
1½ cups unsweetened almond milk
½ cup walnuts
2 tablespoons raw honey
¼ teaspoon vanilla extract
1 tablespoon freshly squeezed lemon juice
¼ teaspoon cinnamon (plus ⅛ teaspoon to garnish)

1. Place all ingredients in blender, except for the reserved cinnamon garnish, and blend on high until smooth.
2. Pour smoothie in a glass and garnish with half of the reserved cinnamon. Enjoy!

NUTRITIONAL INFORMATION (PER SERVING SIZE):

CALORIES:	CARBOHYDRATES:	PROTEIN:	FAT:	SODIUM:	FIBER:	SUGAR:
382.25 (kcal)	67.5 (g)	7.25 (g)	21.5 (g)	320 (mg)	16.75 (g)	82.5 (g)

Peaches and Cream Smoothie

This creamy and sweet glass of goodness is rich, thick, full of flavor, and completely mouth-watering. In this smoothie, peaches, coconut milk, bananas, and honey come together in harmony, making for a perfectly balanced drink. You will find that the creaminess of the canned coconut milk chilled overnight, and the sweet notes of the fresh and ripened peaches, create a smoothie that is both delectable and healthy. It is a wonderful treat to have on a sunny morning or sunny afternoon, as it'll refresh you and provide you with a nice energy boost. This Peaches and Cream Smoothie is sure to satisfy the strongest of cravings, so feel free to indulge!

Time: 5 minutes | **Difficulty:** Easy | **Yields:** 16 ounces | **Serving size:** 8 ounces

1½ frozen bananas
2 ripe peaches, pitted
½ cup unsweetened coconut milk (from carton, not canned)
½ cup canned coconut milk, chilled overnight
1 tablespoon raw honey

Place all ingredients in blender and blend on high until smooth.

NUTRITIONAL INFORMATION (PER SERVING SIZE):

CALORIES:	CARBOHYDRATES:	PROTEIN:	FAT:	SODIUM:	FIBER:	SUGAR:
293.25 (kcal)	65.5 (g)	3.75 (g)	13 (g)	26.5 (mg)	13.5 (g)	62 (g)

Maple Pecan Smoothie

This Paleo recipe features soaked pecans mixed with bananas, almond milk, a bit of maple syrup, and some spices, ingredients that give this Maple Pecan Smoothie a sweet refreshing flavor. This combination of pecans, bananas, and almond milk makes this smoothie an extremely healthy alternative to pecan pie, one of the worst pies for you. Now, not only are you able to enjoy a sweet treat, you won't have to feel guilty about eating a fat- and calorie-laden dessert. Your body *and* taste buds will thank you!

Time: 5 minutes | **Difficulty:** Easy | **Yields:** 16 ounces | **Serving size:** 8 ounces

2 frozen bananas
1½ cups unsweetened vanilla almond milk
½ cup pecans, soaked in water overnight
  (drain water before using)
2 tablespoons maple syrup
¼ teaspoon vanilla extract
⅛ teaspoon nutmeg
⅛ teaspoon cinnamon

Place all ingredients in blender and blend on high until smooth.

NUTRITIONAL INFORMATION (PER SERVING SIZE):

CALORIES:	CARBOHYDRATES:	PROTEIN:	FAT:	SODIUM:	FIBER:	SUGAR:
378.05 (kcal)	45.63 (g)	4.25 (g)	22 (g)	276 (mg)	12.75 (g)	54.5 (g)

Old-Fashioned Vanilla Smoothie

This Old-Fashioned Vanilla Smoothie is full of flavorful vanilla and coconut notes that are sure to make your heart sing. With just a sip of this creamy vanilla concoction, you'll be taken back to those hot summer days where playing under the sun and swimming for hours was the norm, times when your parents would treat you to a nice, cold vanilla shake to make your day that much better! This drink is very much like those decadent vanilla shakes—only better. The added flavor from the shredded coconut and bananas make it extra scrumptious, and its all-natural ingredient list makes this a very healthy treat!

Time: 5 minutes | **Difficulty:** Easy | **Yields:** 16 ounces | **Serving size:** 8 ounces

2 frozen bananas
1½ cups unsweetened almond milk
¼ cup unsweetened shredded coconut
1 tablespoon maple syrup
¼ teaspoon vanilla extract
¼ teaspoon cinnamon
⅛ teaspoon sea salt

Place all ingredients in blender and blend on high until smooth.

NUTRITIONAL INFORMATION (PER SERVING SIZE):

CALORIES:	CARBOHYDRATES:	PROTEIN:	FAT:	SODIUM:	FIBER:	SUGAR:
229.25 (kcal)	38.1 (g)	2.35 (g)	9 (g)	280.8 (mg)	10.55 (g)	41.7 (g)

Detox Smoothies

Do you ever get the feeling that your body needs a food break? That all that bacon you've been feeding it is just too heavy and too greasy, and that at the moment your body needs to stay away from all solids? Well, even followers of the Paleo diet should give their bodies a little break here and there. A body detoxification or "detox" is the process of removing toxic substances or qualities from the body. In a world where most foods have been processed and genetically modified, every once in a while your body wants to be taken through small detox periods where you only ingest water and nutritious liquids. Fruit and vegetable smoothies will provide you with lots of great detox-friendly nutrients to help you achieve your detoxification goal. With these healthy drinks, you'll give your body vitamin C, carotenoids, flavonoids, glutathione, and citrus pectin, among other great nutrients, which do a wonderful job in helping you detoxify. Fortunately, Detox Smoothies like the Sunflower Healing Smoothie, the Pumpkin Ginger Smoothie, and the Açaí Boost Smoothie in this section will keep your detoxification goals on track and will make it easier for you to stick to them. And, unlike other detox recipes, these smoothies are not only very tasty, but they also keep you full and content for long periods of time. So give these a try and see how you feel. If your body could talk after drinking some of these, it would say something like: "You're my hero!"

Detoxify Smoothie

With all of the foods you likely consume—both healthy and unhealthy—your body is constantly collecting toxins. Fortunately, this smoothie is full of raspberries, pear, and other all-natural ingredients that are sure to help your body detoxify. Raspberries contain antioxidants that can help slow the aging process and protect the body against free radicals that can cause diseases and even cancer. They also contain potassium, which can support healthy blood pressure and an overall healthy heart. Pears include a significant amount of fiber that aids in digestion and can help your body flush toxins out of the digestive tract. Mixing these two special ingredients with the others included in this recipe will help you detox in no time!

Time: 5 minutes | **Difficulty:** Easy | **Yields:** 20 ounces | **Serving size:** 10 ounces

1½ cups frozen raspberries
1 ripe pear, cored
½ avocado
1 cup baby kale
1½ cups unsweetened almond milk
1 tablespoon raw honey

Place all ingredients in blender and blend on high until smooth.

NUTRITIONAL INFORMATION (PER SERVING SIZE):

CALORIES:	CARBOHYDRATES:	PROTEIN:	FAT:	SODIUM:	FIBER:	SUGAR:
250 (kcal)	40 (g)	4 (g)	10.5 (g)	310 (mg)	26 (g)	40.5 (g)

Back to Basics Smoothie

Do you tend to get caught up in the hustle and bustle of life and watch as the world starts to pass you by? If you do, sometimes it's good to step back and realize that the sweetest things in life are simple. This Back to Basics Smoothie is a simple reminder that enjoyable things in life don't have to be flashy or extravagant. With the perfect mix of pineapple, mango, coconut water, and some greens, you can enjoy an all-natural treat that tastes amazing and feeds your body fiber and a number of beneficial vitamins and minerals. It will help you detox and unwind, and its health benefits will improve your quality of life. So mix up this delicious Paleo smoothie, and remember that there is beauty in simplicity.

Time: 5 minutes | **Difficulty:** Easy | **Yields:** 20 ounces | **Serving size:** 10 ounces

1 cup frozen pineapple chunks
1 cup frozen mango slices
1 cup spinach
½ cup kale
1½ cups coconut water

Place all ingredients in blender and blend on high until smooth.

NUTRITIONAL INFORMATION (PER SERVING SIZE):

CALORIES:	CARBOHYDRATES:	PROTEIN:	FAT:	SODIUM:	FIBER:	SUGAR:
140.75 (kcal)	33.95 (g)	3.5 (g)	0 (g)	97.5 (mg)	11 (g)	49 (g)

Blackberry Forest Smoothie

Blackberries not only make salads and smoothies more delicious, but they are also full of nutrients. They have one of the highest fiber contents of any plant in the world, which means that they help with digestion and keep toxins from sitting idle in your digestive system. Blackberries are also low in calories, which makes them a delicious and healthy alternative to many sugary snacks you find in the grocery store. In addition, blackberries contain anthocyanins, an antioxidant that can help reduce inflammation, and vitamin C, which helps support a healthy immune system and protects you from sickness and disease. This natural berry adds great taste when blended into a smoothie, so whirl all of the goodness together and enjoy a healthy and delicious treat!

Time: 5 minutes | **Difficulty:** Easy | **Yields:** 20 ounces | **Serving size:** 10 ounces

½ cup frozen blackberries
2 frozen bananas
1 cup baby spinach
¼ avocado
1¼ cups unsweetened almond milk
Juice of ½ lemon
1 teaspoon almond flour (to garnish)

1. Place all ingredients in blender, except for the almond flour, and blend on high until smooth.
2. Pour smoothie in a glass and garnish with half of the almond flour. Enjoy!

NUTRITIONAL INFORMATION (PER SERVING SIZE):

CALORIES:	CARBOHYDRATES:	PROTEIN:	FAT:	SODIUM:	FIBER:	SUGAR:
205.75 (kcal)	36.1 (g)	3.63 (g)	7 (g)	255 (mg)	16 (g)	32.4 (g)

Blueberry Dream Smoothie

The amazing blueberries used in this recipe give this Blueberry Dream Smoothie its unique flavor. Blueberries have a lot to offer in terms of nutrients as well. Blueberries have been shown to slow down vision loss, and with more antioxidants than any other fruit or vegetable, this berry is a delicious and healthy snack to have on its own or to mix into your Paleo smoothie. In addition, blueberries contain antioxidant chemical compounds called polyphenols that can break down belly fat, help your metabolism, and aid in the neutralization of free radicals that could damage your cells. If you want a low-calorie snack, these are the berries for you, with less than 100 calories for a full cup. Enjoy!

Time: 5 minutes | **Difficulty:** Easy | **Yields:** 20 ounces | **Serving size:** 10 ounces

1 cup frozen blueberries
1 frozen banana
1 cup kale
1½ cups unsweetened almond milk
1 tablespoon almond butter
¼ teaspoon cinnamon
1 teaspoon chia seeds

Place all ingredients in blender and blend on high until smooth.

NUTRITIONAL INFORMATION (PER SERVING SIZE):

CALORIES:	CARBOHYDRATES:	PROTEIN:	FAT:	SODIUM:	FIBER:	SUGAR:
203.65 (kcal)	31.75 (g)	4.1 (g)	7.5 (g)	303.8 (mg)	12.55 (g)	29 (g)

Açaí Boost Smoothie

What's all of this talk about açaí? Although açaí berries have been around for a long time, they are gaining popularity due to their powerful health benefits. Açaí berries are found primarily in the Amazon and are extremely high in anthocyanins, antioxidants that lower cholesterol levels in the blood. Apart from acting as wonderful antioxidants, the anthocyanins found in açaí berries help you fight against free radicals and offer anti-viral, anti-inflammatory, and anti-cancer benefits. Antioxidants are an extremely important part of the ongoing detoxification process, helping your body flush out unwanted toxins. Açaí berries have also been shown to help with weight loss and skin health; may provide potential energy boosts, better sex, improved mental function, and anti-aging properties; and may also help your body avoid the side effects of oxidative damage. Try adding some juice from this amazing berry to your Paleo smoothie and enjoy its taste—and health benefits!

Time: 5 minutes | **Difficulty:** Easy | **Yields:** 20 ounces | **Serving size:** 10 ounces

1 frozen banana
1½ cups frozen blueberries
½ cup fresh coconut meat
1½ cups organic açaí juice

Place all ingredients in blender and blend on high until smooth.

NUTRITIONAL INFORMATION (PER SERVING SIZE):

CALORIES:	CARBOHYDRATES:	PROTEIN:	FAT:	SODIUM:	FIBER:	SUGAR:
187.25 (kcal)	32.25 (g)	1.9 (g)	7 (g)	10.5 (mg)	12.5 (g)	39 (g)

Caribbean Sunset Smoothie

Do you ever wish you were in the Caribbean, enjoying life by the sea, sipping on a sweet tropical drink with one of those little umbrella straws? If today is one of those days, where you just can't help but daydream about a tropical paradise, then you've come to the right place! This smoothie recipe will satisfy your craving for the tropics, providing you with a splash of sweet, sweet paradise. The blend of banana, strawberries, papaya, and orange juice create an all-natural fruit mixture that carries your senses away to a place of pure bliss. Your body will rejoice with so much goodness!

Time: 5 minutes | **Difficulty:** Easy | **Yields:** 24 ounces | **Serving size:** 8 ounces

1 frozen banana
1 cup frozen strawberries
1 cup ripe papaya
1½ cups orange juice, preferably freshly squeezed

Place all ingredients in blender and blend on high until smooth.

NUTRITIONAL INFORMATION (PER SERVING SIZE):

CALORIES:	CARBOHYDRATES:	PROTEIN:	FAT:	SODIUM:	FIBER:	SUGAR:
125.67 (kcal)	30.7 (g)	1.5 (g)	0 (g)	10 (mg)	9 (g)	60.5 (g)

Can't Beet This Smoothie

Although the beet probably isn't the first thing that comes to mind when wanting to add flavor to your smoothie, it's hard to beat the beet in terms of nutrition. Beets are full of vitamins and minerals, including magnesium, potassium, phosphorus, iron, beta-carotene, betacyanin, and vitamins A, B, and C. These vitamins and minerals help cleanse your liver and purify the blood. Beets are also full of fiber, which can help the digestive system remove toxins and waste. They have also been shown to boost immunity and protect your body against cancer. Beets are a very low-calorie food and can even help tame your sweet tooth, so drink up!

Time: 5 minutes | **Difficulty:** Easy | **Yields:** 16 ounces | **Serving size:** 8 ounces

1 beet
1½ cups frozen blueberries
1 seedless orange, peeled
1 cup unsweetened almond milk
3 Medjool dates, pitted

1. Place beet in a juicer and follow its instructions. Use the juice only and discard the pulp.
2. Place all ingredients in blender and blend on high until smooth.

NUTRITIONAL INFORMATION (PER SERVING SIZE):

CALORIES:	CARBOHYDRATES:	PROTEIN:	FAT:	SODIUM:	FIBER:	SUGAR:
221.25 (kcal)	52.5 (g)	3 (g)	1.5 (g)	218.25 (mg)	15.25 (g)	85 (g)

Can You Say Cilantro Smoothie

What is small, green, and has a distinct fresh taste that is common in salsas and many other recipes? You guessed it, cilantro! This herb is an anti-inflammatory that is rich in magnesium, iron, and phytonutrients, and acts as a natural and powerful cleansing and detoxifying agent within the body. Believe it or not, metals like mercury can make their way into the tissues of your body through foods you eat, like river and ocean fish. Lucky, the chemical compounds within cilantro can actually help remove these metals. Cilantro is also cholesterol-free and is rich in antioxidants that can help reduce free radicals in the body. In addition, the iron in cilantro is essential for red blood cell production and can help overall cardiovascular health. Mix this little herb with some pineapple, banana, and almond milk to get a uniquely healthy Paleo smoothie that is sure to brighten your day!

Time: 5 minutes | **Difficulty:** Easy | **Yields:** 20 ounces | **Serving size:** 10 ounces

1 cup frozen pineapple chunks
1 frozen banana
1 cup seedless green grapes
1 tablespoon chopped cilantro
1 cup unsweetened vanilla almond milk
1 tablespoon raw honey

Place all ingredients in blender and blend on high until smooth.

NUTRITIONAL INFORMATION (PER SERVING SIZE):

CALORIES:	CARBOHYDRATES:	PROTEIN:	FAT:	SODIUM:	FIBER:	SUGAR:
157 (kcal)	36 (g)	1.5 (g)	1.5 (g)	187 (mg)	5 (g)	54.5 (g)

Grapefull Smoothie

What are you "grapeful" for? This Grapefull Smoothie, of course! The grapefruit juice that anchors this recipe is really something to take seriously. It packs a punch of nutrients and minerals that your body is starved for! Although you may think of grapefruit as bitter, when mixed with some sweeter fruits like bananas and oranges, it really complements the overall taste of your Paleo creation. Get the nourishment you need and satisfy your body's thirst for nutrition!

Time: 5 minutes | **Difficulty:** Easy | **Yields:** 16 ounces | **Serving size:** 8 ounces

1 grapefruit
1½ frozen bananas
½ cup canned coconut milk, chilled overnight
1 cup orange juice, preferably freshly squeezed
2 tablespoons raw honey

1. Place grapefruit in a juicer and follow its instructions. Use the juice only and discard the pulp.
2. Place all ingredients in blender and blend on high until smooth.

NUTRITIONAL INFORMATION (PER SERVING SIZE):

CALORIES:	CARBOHYDRATES:	PROTEIN:	FAT:	SODIUM:	FIBER:	SUGAR:
324.5 (kcal)	76 (g)	3.75 (g)	12 (g)	22 (mg)	11 (g)	86 (g)

Apple Walnut Smoothie

Do the words "apple" and "walnut" get your mouth watering? Then this Apple Walnut Smoothie is just what you need. Delicious *and* healthy, these two foods are great on their own, but the apples are really brought to a new level when mixed with the healthy walnut. Walnuts are packed with antioxidants that can boost your heart health and help protect your body against free radicals. Some studies have even found that the consumption of walnut oil can help protect your body from high blood pressure when stress is introduced. In addition, these crunchy morsels are full of omega-3 fatty acids that have been shown to reduce depression and other negative symptoms. So stop your mouth from watering and mix up this delicious treat now!

Time: 5 minutes | **Difficulty:** Easy | **Yields:** 16 ounces | **Serving size:** 8 ounces

1 red apple
1½ frozen bananas
**¼ cup walnuts, soaked in water overnight
  (drain water before using)**
1 cup unsweetened almond milk
2 Medjool dates, pitted
¼ teaspoon cinnamon

1. Place apple in a juicer and follow its instructions. Use the juice only and discard the pulp.
2. Place all ingredients in blender and blend on high until smooth.

NUTRITIONAL INFORMATION (PER SERVING SIZE):

CALORIES:	CARBOHYDRATES:	PROTEIN:	FAT:	SODIUM:	FIBER:	SUGAR:
232.88 (kcal)	54 (g)	4.25 (g)	11 (g)	184.5 (mg)	16 (g)	57.75 (g)

Sunflower Healing Smoothie

Are you up for a little healing? Not a *treatment* that just looks at the symptoms and ignores root causes, but true *healing*, the kind that starts with detoxing and finishes with giving your body what it needs to repair itself, keeping you strong and healthy. If the answer is yes, then this Sunflower Healing Smoothie is perfect for you! It contains key ingredients—like pears and sunflower seed butter—that give your body the proper nutrition it needs to heal. Mixing these ingredients together gives you a natural and delicious smoothie that provides your body with the nutrients it needs to help you live a healthier and more enjoyable life—and it tastes great, too. Enjoy!

Time: 5 minutes | **Difficulty:** Easy | **Yields:** 16 ounces | **Serving size:** 8 ounces

2 green pears, cored
2 tablespoons organic unsweetened sunflower seed butter
1 cup canned coconut milk, chilled overnight
¼ teaspoon cinnamon
3 coconut water ice cubes

Place all ingredients in blender and blend on high until smooth.

NUTRITIONAL INFORMATION (PER SERVING SIZE):

CALORIES:	CARBOHYDRATES:	PROTEIN:	FAT:	SODIUM:	FIBER:	SUGAR:
430.75 (kcal)	31 (g)	7 (g)	34 (g)	80 (mg)	13.75 (g)	34 (g)

Tahini Twist Smoothie

Just the name of this exotic smoothie—the Tahini Twist Smoothie—is exciting. It's probably because this means that you can taste the flavors of tropical locales *and* because it means that you are about to try something delicious and fruity. Along with the tropical mango, the tahini in this recipe really makes you feel like you're on vacation—and it's healthy too! Tahini actually comes from sesame seeds and is rich in minerals like phosphorus, lecithin, magnesium, potassium, and iron. These minerals help the body by preventing muscle cramps, keeping your bones healthy, and more. Tahini is also a great source of calcium and is high in vitamins B_1, B_2, B_3, B_5, and B_{15}. So mix up this Paleo treat and enjoy that tropical vacation!

Time: 5 minutes | **Difficulty:** Easy | **Yields:** 16 ounces | **Serving size:** 8 ounces

1½ cups frozen mango slices
¼ cup canned coconut milk
1 cup unsweetened coconut milk (from carton, not canned)
1 tablespoon tahini
Juice of ½ lemon

Place all ingredients in blender and blend on high until smooth.

NUTRITIONAL INFORMATION (PER SERVING SIZE):

CALORIES:	CARBOHYDRATES:	PROTEIN:	FAT:	SODIUM:	FIBER:	SUGAR:
203.13 (kcal)	25.25 (g)	2.88 (g)	12.5 (g)	35 (mg)	6.5 (g)	37.5 (g)

Brazil Nuts Smoothie

Brazil is a beautiful country, and thanks to the Brazil nut, this beautiful Paleo smoothie does it justice. This nut is tasty, a great smoothie ingredient, and offers some pretty good nutrition. In fact, the Brazil nut is said to be one of the richest dietary sources of selenium, a powerful antioxidant that can help the body rid itself of free radicals that oxidize body cells and can cause damage. This nut is a great source of essential minerals such as phosphorus, zinc, magnesium, copper, and manganese. Some of these minerals are used to repair tissues, promote healthy bones, and keep your skin healthy. Mix the Brazil nuts with the banana and the other healthy ingredients to create a natural and delicious Paleo smoothie that will taste great, detox your body, and keep you moving throughout the day.

Time: 5 minutes | **Difficulty:** Easy | **Yields:** 20 ounces | **Serving size:** 10 ounces

1 frozen banana
1 cup frozen nectarine slices
¼ cup Brazil nuts, soaked in water overnight (drain water before using)
1½ cups unsweetened almond milk
⅛ teaspoon fresh vanilla beans
1 tablespoon maple syrup

Place all ingredients in blender and blend on high until smooth.

NUTRITIONAL INFORMATION (PER SERVING SIZE):

CALORIES:	CARBOHYDRATES:	PROTEIN:	FAT:	SODIUM:	FIBER:	SUGAR:
248.4 (kcal)	31 (g)	4.13 (g)	13.5 (g)	274 (mg)	9 (g)	39.7 (g)

Strawberry Basil Smoothie

Strawberry and basil are ingredients that you probably don't mix every day, but that's what is so great about smoothies: You can add ingredients without having to worry much about textures playing well together because everything comes out as a delicious liquid. It may seem surprising, but the sweet taste of the strawberries pairs well with the unique flavor of the basil, and that's just the beginning. Basil adds some pretty intense health benefits to the mix! It contains vitamin K, iron, calcium, vitamin C, omega-3 fatty acids, and an array of antioxidants that protect the body against free radicals and cell oxidation. Who knew this simple little green plant had so much to offer? Well, knowledge is power, and now you know! Do enjoy your unique Strawberry Basil Smoothie and bask in all of its flavor and health benefits.

Time: 5 minutes | **Difficulty:** Easy | **Yields:** 16 ounces | **Serving size:** 8 ounces

1½ cups frozen strawberries
8 fresh basil leaves
1½ cups unsweetened coconut milk (from carton, not canned)
2 tablespoons raw honey
Juice of ½ lime

Place all ingredients in blender and blend on high until smooth.

NUTRITIONAL INFORMATION (PER SERVING SIZE):

CALORIES:	CARBOHYDRATES:	PROTEIN:	FAT:	SODIUM:	FIBER:	SUGAR:
138 (kcal)	28.5 (g)	0.75 (g)	3.4 (g)	28 (mg)	6 (g)	47.5 (g)

Pumpkin Ginger Smoothie

Pumpkin is a main ingredient in this Paleo smoothie, but it's the ginger that really steals the show! Ginger is a pretty cool ingredient, not only for its unique flavor but also for the health benefits it has to offer. This spice can actually help your body absorb essential nutrients, which makes it a perfect ingredient to add to an already healthy smoothie. Want to avoid embarrassing situations? Then maybe you should consider ginger as an even more important part of your diet. Ginger can help reduce the buildup of gas in your system!

Time: 5 minutes | **Difficulty:** Easy | **Yields:** 20 ounces | **Serving size:** 10 ounces

1½ frozen bananas
1 cup organic pumpkin purée
1 cup canned coconut milk, chilled overnight
2 teaspoons freshly grated ginger
1 Medjool date, pitted
¼ teaspoon cinnamon

Place all ingredients in blender and blend on high until smooth.

NUTRITIONAL INFORMATION (PER SERVING SIZE):

CALORIES:	CARBOHYDRATES:	PROTEIN:	FAT:	SODIUM:	FIBER:	SUGAR:
379.5 (kcal)	62.25 (g)	5.75 (g)	24.5 (g)	45.25 (mg)	17.95 (g)	66 (g)

Energy Smoothies

You feel great when you're filled with energy, right? You're motivated to get things done. You're fun to be around. You have extra pep in your step.

Yes, energy is important, and you want it to be a natural state of your everyday life from the moment you wake up until the moment you go to bed. But how do you get yourself energized? With proper nutrition, that's how! By ingesting the right ingredients and making sure you stick to a well-balanced diet, you ensure high energy levels and a great sense of well-being. Fortunately, the Energy Smoothies in this section—from the Citrus Drive Smoothie to the Persimmon Pick-Me-Up Smoothie—are guaranteed to improve your liveliness! Be sure to take note of how your body feels after consuming certain ingredients. You'll want to begin recognizing which ingredients your body reacts well to, so you can better feed your body in the future and be the best you can be!

Berry Bomb Smoothie

The boysenberries used in this recipe are a little bigger than blackberries. They have a dark purple color, and are juicy and intense. They are not sold in every grocery store, but they are definitely worth the search. This berry is very high in fiber, and it helps keep your arteries and intestines healthy and clear. It also reduces constipation, heart disease, and hemorrhoids. In addition, boysenberries are a good source of vitamins B and E, which help reduce the risk of heart disease and cancer, provide you with energy, and help your body with cell creation. Cheers!

Time: 5 minutes | **Difficulty:** Easy | **Yields:** 24 ounces | **Serving size:** 8 ounces

½ cup frozen blueberries
½ cup frozen boysenberries
½ cup frozen raspberries
1 frozen banana
1 cup baby kale
2 cups organic unfiltered apple juice

Place all ingredients in blender and blend on high until smooth.

NUTRITIONAL INFORMATION (PER SERVING SIZE):

CALORIES:	CARBOHYDRATES:	PROTEIN:	FAT:	SODIUM:	FIBER:	SUGAR:
175 (kcal)	30 (g)	1.5 (g)	0.17 (g)	81.5 (mg)	13.5 (g)	88.5 (g)

Citrus Drive Smoothie

There is something about the smell of citrus that just awakens the senses; it has a pure freshness about it. Just one whiff can give a burst of energy and get the taste buds tingling. The orange is a pretty amazing citrus fruit. It is juicy and has one of the most wonderful tastes, which means this Citrus Drive Smoothie is out of this world! It mixes the sweet citrus of the orange with raw honey for a sweet pick-me-up that is all natural and loaded with vitamins and minerals. So whether you are fighting a sweet tooth or are just hungry for something delicious, mix this smoothie up and satisfy your cravings!

Time: 5 minutes | **Difficulty:** Easy | **Yields:** 16 ounces | **Serving size:** 8 ounces

1 cup orange juice, preferably freshly squeezed
½ cup canned coconut milk, chilled overnight
2 tablespoons raw honey
¼ teaspoon vanilla extract
5 coconut water ice cubes

Place all ingredients in blender and blend on high until smooth.

NUTRITIONAL INFORMATION (PER SERVING SIZE):

CALORIES:	CARBOHYDRATES:	PROTEIN:	FAT:	SODIUM:	FIBER:	SUGAR:
199.25 (kcal)	24.25 (g)	1.75 (g)	12 (g)	17 (mg)	2 (g)	44.5 (g)

It's Nuts Smoothie

Thanks to the pecans used in this Paleo recipe, the taste and nutritional value of this smoothie is just plain nutty! Pecans aren't just a fun crunchy nut for snacking, they also add many nutrients and some subtle flavor to your smoothies. These little nuts are high in unsaturated fat and can help lower the bad types of cholesterol that can negatively impact blood flow and overall heart health. These little treats are also full of vitamins and minerals, including vitamins A, B, and E; folic acid; calcium; magnesium; phosphorus; potassium; and more. They are also full of antioxidants that help the body keep cancer-causing free radicals under control. All those health benefits *and* it's delicious? Yes! Try it out and go nuts!

Time: 5 minutes | **Difficulty:** Easy | **Yields:** 24 ounces | **Serving size:** 8 ounces

1½ frozen bananas
¼ cup pecans, soaked in water overnight
   (drain water before using)
¼ cup cashews, soaked in water overnight
   (drain water before using)
1½ cups unsweetened almond milk
2 Medjool dates, pitted
¼ teaspoon vanilla extract
¼ teaspoon cinnamon

Place all ingredients in blender and blend on high until smooth.

NUTRITIONAL INFORMATION (PER SERVING SIZE):

CALORIES:	CARBOHYDRATES:	PROTEIN:	FAT:	SODIUM:	FIBER:	SUGAR:
281.3 (kcal)	47.7 (g)	6 (g)	16 (g)	279.5 (mg)	18.75 (g)	80.5 (g)

Fig Vibe Smoothie

Drinking smoothies is a great way to feed your body the nutrients it needs and allow it to more readily absorb the vitamins and minerals it may be missing. This energizing Fig Vibe Smoothie is no exception. Figs are a good source of the mineral potassium, which can help reduce blood pressure and can help you avoid hypertension if you eat a high-sodium diet. Figs are also high in fiber, which is great for the digestive system and weight management, and can help remove toxins and waste in a more efficient and effective manner. High in vitamin C, figs can also help boost your immune system and support healthy bone density. So add this sweet and nutritious ingredient to your smoothie and forget just feeling the "good vibes," because it's time to *actually* feel good!

Time: 5 minutes | **Difficulty:** Easy | **Yields:** 16 ounces | **Serving size:** 8 ounces

1½ frozen bananas
3 ripe figs
2 tablespoons hazelnut butter
1½ cups unsweetened almond milk

Place all ingredients in blender and blend on high until smooth.

NUTRITIONAL INFORMATION (PER SERVING SIZE):

CALORIES:	CARBOHYDRATES:	PROTEIN:	FAT:	SODIUM:	FIBER:	SUGAR:
250.25 (kcal)	54.82 (g)	4.65 (g)	11.5 (g)	275 (mg)	16.3 (g)	64 (g)

Cool Nectarine Smoothie

Nectarines are kind of cool, aren't they? It's amazing that these simple fruits have such an amazing amount of flavor, are refreshingly juicy, are packed with healthy vitamins the body needs, and that there are more than 100 known varieties! In addition, nectarines contain iron, phosphorus, potassium, magnesium, folic acid, vitamin A, vitamin C, vitamin K, and are full of antioxidants. They also contain a lot of fiber and potassium that can help support good heart health, help with digestion, and help remove toxins and waste. What are you waiting for? Whip up this energizing Paleo beverage and enjoy the Cool Nectarine Smoothie!

Time: 5 minutes | **Difficulty:** Easy | **Yields:** 16 ounces | **Serving size:** 8 ounces

1 cup frozen nectarine slices
1 cup frozen strawberries
1 cup orange juice, preferably freshly squeezed
1 teaspoon coconut cream concentrate
1 teaspoon raw honey

Place all ingredients in blender and blend on high until smooth.

NUTRITIONAL INFORMATION (PER SERVING SIZE):

CALORIES:	CARBOHYDRATES:	PROTEIN:	FAT:	SODIUM:	FIBER:	SUGAR:
107.5 (kcal)	23.5 (g)	3 (g)	1.5 (g)	4.5 (mg)	7 (g)	39.7 (g)

Peachy Time Smoothie

The peach is the main ingredient in the Paleo Peachy Time Smoothie, but this recipe wouldn't be as amazing as it is without the addition of the almond milk. Almond milk is a healthy alternative to regular milk, as it is lower in calories and has less cholesterol. Also, almond milk has a significant amount of calcium and vitamin D, which can help support the growth of healthy bones. It also contains vitamin E, which can improve your skin's health. Who doesn't want younger-looking skin? Stay energized and keep your body fed with the proper nutrients it needs with this peachy, creamy, and delicious smoothie!

Time: 5 minutes | **Difficulty:** Easy | **Yields:** 24 ounces | **Serving size:** 8 ounces

1½ cups frozen white peach slices
1 cup frozen blueberries
¼ cup organic carrot purée
1½ cups unsweetened almond milk
2 tablespoons raw honey

Place all ingredients in blender and blend on high until smooth.

NUTRITIONAL INFORMATION (PER SERVING SIZE):

CALORIES:	CARBOHYDRATES:	PROTEIN:	FAT:	SODIUM:	FIBER:	SUGAR:
192.75 (kcal)	29.2 (g)	1.57 (g)	1.5 (g)	283 (mg)	9.1 (g)	53.3 (g)

Coconut Blast Smoothie

This Paleo smoothie truly is a coconut blast. Almost all of the ingredients used in this recipe are coconut-based. With this much coconut, this refreshing smoothie is sure to transport your mind to a tropical island where the birds sing, the sun shines, the waves crash, and the air is fresh. In addition to giving your mind a tropical vacation, coconuts are also packed with nutritional benefits. They can help lower cholesterol, improve digestion, ward off wrinkles, build cells, increase thyroid production, and even increase your metabolism. So if you want to take your mind and taste buds to a warmer climate, mix up this smoothie, pour it in a fun glass, kick up your feet, and enjoy the healthy life.

Time: 5 minutes | **Difficulty:** Easy | **Yields:** 20 ounces | **Serving size:** 10 ounces

1 cup coconut meat
1 cup unsweetened coconut milk (from carton, not canned)
3 tablespoons raw honey
5 coconut water ice cubes
1 tablespoon unsweetened toasted coconut flakes (to garnish)

1. Place all ingredients in blender, except for the toasted coconut flakes, and blend on high until smooth.
2. Pour smoothie in a glass and garnish with half of the coconut flakes. Enjoy!

NUTRITIONAL INFORMATION (PER SERVING SIZE):

CALORIES:	CARBOHYDRATES:	PROTEIN:	FAT:	SODIUM:	FIBER:	SUGAR:
298 (kcal)	36.15 (g)	2.5 (g)	18 (g)	286 (mg)	11.8 (g)	64.8 (g)

Persimmon Pick-Me-Up Smoothie

The persimmon originated in China. It is high in vitamins and minerals such as potassium, magnesium, calcium, iron, and manganese. These vitamins and minerals help with your body's everyday functioning and can help support a strong immune system, which is always good when flu season rolls around! The persimmon also contains high amounts of fiber and antioxidants that aid in digestion and protect your body from free radicals. In addition, consuming one medium-sized portion of this fruit can help fight atherosclerosis, a dangerous disease of the arteries. Mixing this fruit with the other delicious ingredients used in this energizing Paleo smoothie (like orange juice, coconut milk, and raw honey) will give your taste buds the flavor they crave and your body some of the nutrition it needs to keep running. Blend it up for your pick-me-up!

Time: 5 minutes | **Difficulty:** Easy | **Yields:** 16 ounces | **Serving size:** 8 ounces

2 ripe persimmons, leaves removed
½ cup orange juice, preferably freshly squeezed
¼ cup canned coconut milk, chilled overnight
1 tablespoon raw honey
⅛ teaspoon ground ginger
5 coconut water ice cubes

Place all ingredients in blender and blend on high until smooth.

NUTRITIONAL INFORMATION (PER SERVING SIZE):

CALORIES:	CARBOHYDRATES:	PROTEIN:	FAT:	SODIUM:	FIBER:	SUGAR:
240.25 (kcal)	47.1 (g)	2.88 (g)	6 (g)	264.7 (mg)	16 (g)	70 (g)

Minty Mango Smoothie

This very uplifting and reviving drink will take you to a place of bliss. It provides you with a powerful tangy flavor at first, and it leaves you with a nice cool aftertaste. It is one of those beverages best enjoyed on hot summer days or during sunny spring mornings. The mint in this smoothie is not only there to add its wonderful flavor; it also brings you great health benefits. Mint can help soothe your digestive tract when your stomach is in pain, rid your body of toxins, cleanse your stomach, clear up the skin, cleanse your blood, and help eliminate bad breath. It's a powerful little herb, isn't it? So sit back and enjoy this mighty and delightful Paleo smoothie!

Time: 5 minutes | **Difficulty:** Easy | **Yields:** 20 ounces | **Serving size:** 10 ounces

1½ cups ripe mango slices
8 mint leaves
1 teaspoon coconut cream concentrate
2 tablespoons raw honey
Juice of ½ lime
5 coconut water ice cubes

Place all ingredients in blender and blend on high until smooth.

NUTRITIONAL INFORMATION (PER SERVING SIZE):

CALORIES:	CARBOHYDRATES:	PROTEIN:	FAT:	SODIUM:	FIBER:	SUGAR:
184.75 (kcal)	44 (g)	3.25 (g)	1.5 (g)	261 (mg)	7.5 (g)	78.5 (g)

Pink Summer Smoothie

Berries and summer go so perfectly together, don't they? They are all around us during that season and are easily accessible. This Paleo smoothie uses berries to create a refreshing, cooling, delicious, and healthy treat to have during those hot summer months! The coconut cream concentrate in this Pink Summer Smoothie makes it very creamy, the honey makes it nice and sweet, the orange juice gives it a wonderful citrusy flavor, the berries give a tart-sweet taste, and the chia seeds provide you with great energy. It sounds amazing already, right? Just wait till you try it!

Time: 5 minutes | **Difficulty:** Easy | **Yields:** 20 ounces | **Serving size:** 10 ounces

1 cup frozen strawberries
1 cup frozen raspberries
1 cup orange juice, preferably freshly squeezed
1 teaspoon coconut cream concentrate
2 tablespoons raw honey
1 teaspoon chia seeds

Place all ingredients in blender and blend on high until smooth.

NUTRITIONAL INFORMATION (PER SERVING SIZE):

CALORIES:	CARBOHYDRATES:	PROTEIN:	FAT:	SODIUM:	FIBER:	SUGAR:
169.9 (kcal)	37.5 (g)	3.35 (g)	2.75 (g)	7.8 (mg)	14.8 (g)	57 (g)

Papaya Wave Smoothie

Hop on the health wave with papaya, a wonderful tropical fruit! Papaya is not only a very pretty ingredient, but it is also wonderfully nutritious. Papaya has lots of antioxidants that help you fight ailments such as cancer and heart disease, and helps slow aging. It also helps you maintain healthy levels of blood sugar, which allows you to keep good energy throughout your day. Papaya can also help with eye problems and help clear your skin. So let this groovy papaya smoothie take you on a fun ride to better health. Get on the wave!

Time: 5 minutes | **Difficulty:** Easy | **Yields:** 16 ounces | **Serving size:** 8 ounces

1 frozen banana
2 cups ripe papaya chunks
1 tablespoon almond butter
1 tablespoon raw honey
1 teaspoon flaxseed
Juice of 1 lemon
5 coconut water ice cubes

Place all ingredients in blender and blend on high until smooth.

NUTRITIONAL INFORMATION (PER SERVING SIZE):

CALORIES:	CARBOHYDRATES:	PROTEIN:	FAT:	SODIUM:	FIBER:	SUGAR:
225.15 (kcal)	43.65 (g)	3.5 (g)	4.85 (g)	264.7 (mg)	13 (g)	54.5 (g)

Glowing Kale Smoothie

Are you in the mood to glow today? If you are, then this recipe will help you get there! The wonderful nutrients that come from these all-natural ingredients will have a very positive effect on the way you look and feel, and this particular Paleo smoothie will add to your well-being. The kale found in this recipe has lots of calcium, vitamin C, vitamin A, vitamin K, and potassium, which improve bone health, prevent diseases, and boost your immune system. In addition, kale is high in iron, which can support proper liver function and help the body transport oxygen around the body. Kale also boasts a high level of vitamin K, which can help your body protect itself against cancers and keep your bones strong. Be assured you'll glow inside out with this amazing recipe. Drink it with confidence!

Time: 5 minutes | **Difficulty:** Easy | **Yields:** 20 ounces | **Serving size:** 10 ounces

2 frozen bananas
1½ cups baby kale
½ cup canned coconut milk, chilled overnight
1½ cups coconut water
1 teaspoon orange zest
1 tablespoon almond butter
½ teaspoon chia seeds

Place all ingredients in blender and blend on high until smooth.

NUTRITIONAL INFORMATION (PER SERVING SIZE):

CALORIES:	CARBOHYDRATES:	PROTEIN:	FAT:	SODIUM:	FIBER:	SUGAR:
332.7 (kcal)	42.45 (g)	6.43 (g)	17 (g)	116.9 (mg)	13.9 (g)	37 (g)

Lifted Blackberry Smoothie

This blackberry smoothie will lift your spirits—and your energy level! It has great flavor, great texture, and great nutrition! It will keep you happy and feed your body right. There are so many fantastic fruits and vegetables added to this smoothie, but the one that adds the most is the small but very fibrous blackberry. This little berry is a gem, as it is very rich in vitamins, minerals, fiber, and antioxidants, while low on fats, carbohydrates, and calories. Blackberries also combine deliciously with bananas and vanilla, which means your taste buds will be thanking you for this truly fantastic blend. Feel lifted while you enjoy some Paleo liquid goodness!

Time: 5 minutes | **Difficulty:** Easy | **Yields:** 20 ounces | **Serving size:** 10 ounces

1½ cups frozen blackberries
1 frozen banana
1 cup baby spinach
1½ cups unsweetened almond milk
¼ teaspoon vanilla extract
¼ teaspoon cinnamon

Place all ingredients in blender and blend on high until smooth.

NUTRITIONAL INFORMATION (PER SERVING SIZE):

CALORIES:	CARBOHYDRATES:	PROTEIN:	FAT:	SODIUM:	FIBER:	SUGAR:
134.75 (kcal)	27.25 (g)	3.25 (g)	3 (g)	296.5 (mg)	17.75 (g)	24.5 (g)

Green Boost Smoothie

Kiwi, apple, mint, coconuts, and more . . . there are so many fruits and vegetables available to you when it comes to making smoothies that it's hard to pick just one. Fortunately, with this energizing Paleo smoothie, you don't have to choose! Packed with fruits and veggies, this green smoothie is very healthy and can easily be a small meal replacement. For those days when you don't have much time to sit down and eat, just prepare this recipe, put it in a to-go cup, and take it along with you! And, if you feel like you need a little goodness in your smoothie, feel free to add more fruits and veggies to your blender!

Time: 5 minutes | **Difficulty:** Easy | **Yields:** 16 ounces | **Serving size:** 8 ounces

1 frozen banana
1 kiwi, peeled
1 green apple, cored
1 cup baby kale
½ cup canned coconut milk, chilled overnight
1 cup coconut water
2 mint leaves (to garnish)

1. Place all ingredients in blender, except for the mint leaves, and blend on high until smooth.
2. Pour smoothie in a glass and garnish with a mint leaf. Enjoy!

NUTRITIONAL INFORMATION (PER SERVING SIZE):

CALORIES:	CARBOHYDRATES:	PROTEIN:	FAT:	SODIUM:	FIBER:	SUGAR:
264.75 (kcal)	39 (g)	4.25 (g)	12 (g)	300 (mg)	13 (g)	42.5 (g)

Cacao Walnut Smoothie

Yum! You have a rich and nice treat with this recipe. If you like chocolate and love a bit of crunch along with it, then this smoothie is for you. The pure cacao powder mixed with fresh dates and cinnamon make for a lovely dessert-like drink. Just add fresh raw walnuts to it, and you've got yourself a treat that is out of this world. To add to its decadence, this smoothie also carries two types of fresh fruits: bananas and boysenberries! This is the type of smoothie you'll want to have after a workout, or on one of those afternoons when you want to treat yourself to something lovely. Treat yourself to this very satisfying, filling, and energizing smoothie!

Time: 5 minutes | **Difficulty:** Easy | **Yields:** 20 ounces | **Serving size:** 10 ounces

2 frozen bananas
¼ cup frozen boysenberries
¼ cup walnuts
1½ cups unsweetened almond milk
1 tablespoon cacao powder
3 Medjool dates, pitted
¼ teaspoon cinnamon (to garnish)

1. Place all ingredients in blender, except for the cinnamon, and blend on high until smooth.
2. Pour smoothie in a glass and garnish with half of the cinnamon. Enjoy!

NUTRITIONAL INFORMATION (PER SERVING SIZE):

CALORIES:	CARBOHYDRATES:	PROTEIN:	FAT:	SODIUM:	FIBER:	SUGAR:
349.38 (kcal)	62 (g)	5.38 (g)	12.5 (g)	274.5 (mg)	18.75 (g)	80.5 (g)

Three-Ingredient Smoothies

Some of the most delicious Paleo smoothies are made out of very few ingredients, and as with the three-ingredient smoothies in this section, each ingredient plays an important role and really gets a chance to shine. But if you're only going to include three ingredients, it's important to know which ingredients mix well with others and which ingredients will take your three-ingredient smoothie to the next level! Developing three-ingredient smoothies means putting your creative cap on and coming up with a variety of great-tasting combinations. Don't be shy; allow yourself to go a little wild and combine all sorts of flavors and textures together. Who knows, you might just happen to create the best smoothie ever blended . . . you really never know what you're missing until you try, right? In this section, you will find a variety of delicious three-ingredient smoothie recipes including the Perfect Three Smoothie, the Hidden Goodness Smoothie, and the Melon Mania Smoothie. So dive on in and get started on your creative three-ingredient journey!

Note: To ensure that your three ingredients are well combined, there is nothing like good ol' trial and error. You'll want to add 1–2 solid fruits or vegetables (frozen or fresh, either one works), some sort of liquid (juice, milk, water, etc.), and a fun choice of your favorite smoothie additive (nut/seed butters, oils, seeds, natural sweeteners, etc.). Enjoy!

Crazy Mango Smoothie

Get ready for an explosion of flavor, because this Crazy Mango Smoothie has a surplus of it! The mango in this recipe is not only crazy delicious, but it is also crazy good for you. Mangos are full of vitamins A, C, and E, which help protect your body against free radicals, support healthy bone growth, boost the immune system, and fight colds. The potassium in mango will help you with proper nerve function and healthy muscle contraction, and the fiber will help you improve your digestion. Mangos are a great smoothie ingredient because they allow for a very smooth consistency when blended, which is so desirable in these types of drinks. Make sure you use very ripe mangos for your smoothie recipes, as that's when they are the sweetest. So take a sip of this Crazy Mango Smoothie and have a crazy-fun day filled with great energy and health!

Time: 5 minutes | **Difficulty:** Easy | **Yields:** 20 ounces | **Serving size:** 10 ounces

1 cup frozen pineapple chunks
1 cup ripe mango slices
1 cup canned coconut milk, chilled overnight

Place all ingredients in blender and blend on high until smooth.

NUTRITIONAL INFORMATION (PER SERVING SIZE):

CALORIES:	CARBOHYDRATES:	PROTEIN:	FAT:	SODIUM:	FIBER:	SUGAR:
317 (kcal)	28 (g)	3.5 (g)	24 (g)	35 (mg)	5 (g)	40 (g)

Tropical Sunrise Smoothie

This lively three-ingredient smoothie will awaken and satisfy you. The apricot-mango juice, the peaches, and the banana create a sweet and tangy flavor that is unique and simply delightful. Doesn't the sound of that fruit combination just make your mouth water? Just wait until you taste it! Apart from these ingredients being delicious, they bring an array of great nutrients to the table; your body will benefit from fiber; zinc; potassium; magnesium; vitamins A, C, E, and K; and antioxidants. This concoction is a perfect breakfast or snack option as it's light and easy to drink. Be adventurous and bring some tropical flavors to your life!

Time: 5 minutes | **Difficulty:** Easy | **Yields:** 20 ounces | **Serving size:** 10 ounces

1 frozen banana
1 cup frozen peach slices
2 cups organic apricot-mango juice

Place all ingredients in blender and blend on high until smooth.

NUTRITIONAL INFORMATION (PER SERVING SIZE):

CALORIES:	CARBOHYDRATES:	PROTEIN:	FAT:	SODIUM:	FIBER:	SUGAR:
212.5 (kcal)	52 (g)	1 (g)	0 (g)	31 (mg)	5 (g)	77 (g)

Hidden Goodness Smoothie

Okay, it's not every day that you run into a smoothie that has broccoli in it. Yes, broccoli! It's a great vegetable to add to your diet because it is a good source of vitamin D, which helps your bones with calcium absorption. It also contains two different kinds of carotenoids that help your vision, and fiber that promotes a healthy digestive system. Broccoli helps reduce cholesterol, it provides three phytonutrients that help you to detox, and it is a good source of protein. You just gotta love this green! In addition, adding greens to your smoothies is a great way to "dress up" or "hide" veggies in meals. The sweet bananas and the deliciously tangy pineapple do a fantastic job at helping disguise the broccoli in your Paleo smoothie. So give it a try! You're guaranteed to love it, and your family will benefit from having broccoli in their lives!

Time: 5 minutes | **Difficulty:** Easy | **Yields:** 20 ounces | **Serving size:** 10 ounces

2 frozen bananas
2 cups pineapple chunks
2 cups broccoli florets

Place all ingredients in blender and blend on high until smooth.

NUTRITIONAL INFORMATION (PER SERVING SIZE):

CALORIES:	CARBOHYDRATES:	PROTEIN:	FAT:	SODIUM:	FIBER:	SUGAR:
218 (kcal)	55 (g)	5 (g)	0 (g)	66 (mg)	14 (g)	64 (g)

Banana Almond Smoothie

You can't lose with a drink that's both creamy and nutty like this Banana Almond Smoothie! The bananas sweeten the recipe and also provide a nice creamy feel. The almonds bring a bold nutty flavor to the mix and give every bite a bit of added crunch. You'll love how you can savor both the almond and the banana flavors with every sip, and you'll go crazy over the wonderful almond aroma this Paleo smoothie exudes. Also, if you are an active person, you'll be happy to get the added potassium for proper muscle function and the manganese to keep your bones healthy.

Time: 5 minutes | **Difficulty:** Easy | **Yields:** 24 ounces | **Serving size:** 8 ounces

2 frozen bananas
2 cups unsweetened vanilla almond milk
2 tablespoons almond butter

Place all ingredients in blender and blend on high until smooth.

NUTRITIONAL INFORMATION (PER SERVING SIZE):

CALORIES:	CARBOHYDRATES:	PROTEIN:	FAT:	SODIUM:	FIBER:	SUGAR:
164 (kcal)	21.3 (g)	2.7 (g)	8.3 (g)	366 (mg)	10 (g)	28 (g)

Melon Mania Smoothie

This reviving smoothie is a great morning drink, especially if you're an early bird. You know those mornings when the sun is rising and the house is still quiet? You may enjoy those moments when everyone else is asleep and you can savor the tranquility all to yourself. If you take those mornings and add this delicate, reviving drink to them, you'll have a little piece of heaven. This Paleo smoothie makes melon the star of the show; it will give you strength and boost your immune system, keeping you healthy and vital. Cheers to melon and to those quiet mornings to yourself.

Time: 5 minutes | **Difficulty:** Easy | **Yields:** 20 ounces | **Serving size:** 10 ounces

2 frozen cups honeydew melon
1½ cups unsweetened coconut milk (from carton, not canned)
2 tablespoons raw honey

Place all ingredients in blender and blend on high until smooth.

NUTRITIONAL INFORMATION (PER SERVING SIZE):

CALORIES:	CARBOHYDRATES:	PROTEIN:	FAT:	SODIUM:	FIBER:	SUGAR:
158.75 (kcal)	33.5 (g)	1 (g)	3.4 (g)	86.5 (mg)	3.5 (g)	64.5 (g)

Perfect Three Smoothie

Prepare for the treat of a lifetime. Blueberries, bananas, or apples may not seem like anything out of the ordinary, but put these three ingredients together, and magic happens. This Perfect Three Smoothie really is one of the yummiest, most satisfying drinks you'll ever taste because each one of these three ingredients brings something special to the table. The bananas give this Paleo smoothie its creamy consistency; the blueberries give it its purple color and its sweet, tart taste; and the unfiltered apple juice combines it all together and adds an extra punch of sweetness. Enjoy perfection!

Time: 5 minutes | **Difficulty:** Easy | **Yields:** 20 ounces | **Serving size:** 10 ounces

2 frozen bananas
1½ cups frozen blueberries
2 cups organic unfiltered apple juice

Place all ingredients in blender and blend on high until smooth.

NUTRITIONAL INFORMATION (PER SERVING SIZE):

CALORIES:	CARBOHYDRATES:	PROTEIN:	FAT:	SODIUM:	FIBER:	SUGAR:
309 (kcal)	57.75 (g)	1.57 (g)	0 (g)	53.5 (mg)	12 (g)	110.5 (g)

Orange Pomegranate Smoothie

You should be glad to have this wonderful fruit available to you year round! Oranges make a wonderful snack; a delicious and thirst-quenching juice; a great smoothie addition; and a wonderful, tangy additive for multiple recipes. This fruit is widely consumed around the world, and there is no question as to why. Oranges mix very well with most fruits and vegetables, but for this particular Paleo smoothie you'll use pomegranates and bananas. Delicious!

Time: 5 minutes | **Difficulty:** Easy | **Yields:** 20 ounces | **Serving size:** 10 ounces

2 frozen bananas
2 seedless oranges, peeled
1½ cups organic pomegranate juice

Place all ingredients in blender and blend on high until smooth.

NUTRITIONAL INFORMATION (PER SERVING SIZE):

CALORIES:	CARBOHYDRATES:	PROTEIN:	FAT:	SODIUM:	FIBER:	SUGAR:
250.5 (kcal)	62.75 (g)	2.75 (g)	0.75 (g)	35 (mg)	10 (g)	94 (g)

Strawberry Date Smoothie

If you're looking to sweeten up your Paleo smoothie, look no further than the humble date! This little ingredient will bring great flavor to your smoothie creations, and it will boost your health too. The date's benefits range from relieving constipation to helping you strengthen your bones. Dates also serve as a good hangover cure, as they have been said to have an effect of absorption and relief. Dates contain calcium, iron, phosphorus, potassium, magnesium, zinc, and an array of vitamins such as A and K. Their higher sugar content makes for a nice all-natural instant energy booster to help get you through a 60-minute workout class or a kids' soccer game. Whenever you may need an extra push, you can always count on your dates! *Note: When you're shopping for these little fruits, make sure you get the ones found in the fresh produce section of the store, not in the bulk and dried-fruit section, as the dates sold in bulk might have added sugars in them.*

Time: 5 minutes | **Difficulty:** Easy | **Yields:** 16 ounces | **Serving size:** 8 ounces

2 cups frozen strawberries
1½ cups unsweetened almond milk
4 Medjool dates, pitted

Place all ingredients in blender and blend on high until smooth.

NUTRITIONAL INFORMATION (PER SERVING SIZE):

CALORIES:	CARBOHYDRATES:	PROTEIN:	FAT:	SODIUM:	FIBER:	SUGAR:
217.5 (kcal)	50.5 (g)	2.75 (g)	2.25 (g)	275 (mg)	14.5 (g)	80 (g)

Cranberry Mango Smoothie

This three-ingredient concoction will appeal to all of your senses. The drink smells amazing, tastes amazing, and feels amazing. There is something great about combining the fragrant mango with the sweet coconut milk and the tart cranberries; the combination is pure culinary magic. The cranberry juice that this recipe calls for has an array of health benefits for both men and women. Cranberry juice helps prevent prostate cancer and urinary tract infections in men; its antioxidants keep free radicals from harming the cells and changing their DNA. It also helps women by providing soothing relief for menstrual cramps. This Cranberry Mango Smoothie is easy to make and easy to drink. Quick and delicious relief is on the way!

Time: 5 minutes | **Difficulty:** Easy | **Yields:** 20 ounces | **Serving size:** 10 ounces

1½ cups frozen mango slices
1½ cups organic cranberry juice
½ cup canned coconut milk, chilled overnight

Place all ingredients in blender and blend on high until smooth.

NUTRITIONAL INFORMATION (PER SERVING SIZE):

CALORIES:	CARBOHYDRATES:	PROTEIN:	FAT:	SODIUM:	FIBER:	SUGAR:
277.75 (kcal)	45.5 (g)	2.75 (g)	12 (g)	27 (mg)	4.5 (g)	82 (g)

Sweet Peach Smoothie

Sweet peaches, bananas, and apple juice. What a combination! This drink recipe will remind you of those lovely summer days where playing all day outside seems like the norm. After all, nothing yells summer more than peaches and apples, so you'll be able to find this smoothie's ingredients very easily at your local co-ops, farmers' market, or grocery store. In addition to their nostalgic taste, peaches bring an array of great antioxidants, calcium, fiber, potassium, and vitamins to the table, so even though they are a smaller low-calorie fruit, they have a lot to offer. In addition, the fiber and potassium found in peaches helps reduce kidney disease, inflammation, and heartburn. Peaches are also very good for your complexion, helping reduce wrinkles and unwanted fine lines. So welcome this plump and colorful fruit to your diet, and add loads of good flavor to those summer days!

Time: 5 minutes | **Difficulty:** Easy | **Yields:** 20 ounces | **Serving size:** 10 ounces

2 cups frozen peach slices
1 frozen banana
1½ cups organic unfiltered apple juice

Place all ingredients in blender and blend on high until smooth.

NUTRITIONAL INFORMATION (PER SERVING SIZE):

CALORIES:	CARBOHYDRATES:	PROTEIN:	FAT:	SODIUM:	FIBER:	SUGAR:
217.5 (kcal)	39.75 (g)	1.5 (g)	0 (g)	38.5 (mg)	7 (g)	61 (g)

Almond Pear Smoothie

Ah, pears and almonds. What a fresh combination: light, elegant, decadent. Even though this Almond Pear Smoothie is very simple, it is plenty satisfying. The bananas add a nice creamy consistency to the smoothie, while the pears add in a splash of flavor. But the really amazing ingredient here is the almond milk. It's great to be able to add "milk" to your Paleo lifestyle without having to add dairy! Almond milk allows for that nice creamy feel that you love, it is a low-calorie option, and it doesn't have any saturated fats, trans fats, or cholesterol. You won't even miss the milk! *Note: when buying almond milk at the store, be sure to pick the unsweetened kind—the purer, the better.*

Time: 5 minutes | **Difficulty:** Easy | **Yields:** 16 ounces | **Serving size:** 8 ounces

1½ frozen bananas
2 pears, cored
1 cup unsweetened vanilla almond milk

Place all ingredients in blender and blend on high until smooth.

NUTRITIONAL INFORMATION (PER SERVING SIZE):

CALORIES:	CARBOHYDRATES:	PROTEIN:	FAT:	SODIUM:	FIBER:	SUGAR:
184.75 (kcal)	64.5 (g)	3 (g)	1.5 (g)	185 (mg)	20 (g)	72 (g)

Apricot and Sweet Potato Smoothie

If you want to feed your body by providing it with wonderful health benefits and sustained energy on those days when you need an extra push, then this Apricot and Sweet Potato Smoothie is the perfect drink! Not only is this sweet smoothie very nourishing, it also puts an end to your cravings and is the perfect afternoon treat! So instead of a bowl full of ice cream, prepare yourself this blended treat. You'll love its taste and how great you'll feel after drinking it.

Time: 5 minutes | **Difficulty:** Easy | **Yields:** 16 ounces | **Serving size:** 8 ounces

1½ frozen bananas
1 cooked sweet potato, peeled
1 cup organic apricot nectar juice

Place all ingredients in blender and blend on high until smooth.

NUTRITIONAL INFORMATION (PER SERVING SIZE):

CALORIES:	CARBOHYDRATES:	PROTEIN:	FAT:	SODIUM:	FIBER:	SUGAR:
200.75 (kcal)	70.5 (g)	2.95 (g)	0.1 (g)	52 (mg)	14.5 (g)	83 (g)

Simple Raspberry Smoothie

A raspberry can speak for itself in terms of flavor; it's one of those fruits that can make a statement with its sweet-tart taste. It mixes really well with other fruits and vegetables, but this Simple Raspberry Smoothie lets the raspberry shine! In order to make this smoothie great, this bright-colored berry is combined with creamy canned coconut milk and with raw honey, the purest of sweeteners. Neither of these ingredients can even compete with the tart, juicy taste of this small-but-strong berry! Make this delicious Paleo smoothie and take the time to soak in its wonderful benefits.

Time: 5 minutes | **Difficulty:** Easy | **Yields:** 12 ounces | **Serving size:** 12 ounces

1 cup frozen raspberries
1 cup canned coconut milk, chilled overnight
3 tablespoons raw honey

Place all ingredients in blender and blend on high until smooth.

NUTRITIONAL INFORMATION (PER SERVING SIZE):

CALORIES:	CARBOHYDRATES:	PROTEIN:	FAT:	SODIUM:	FIBER:	SUGAR:
701 (kcal)	69 (g)	6 (g)	49 (g)	34 (mg)	8 (g)	57.5 (g)

Berry Mix Smoothie

This Berry Mix Smoothie is an antioxidant haven, where a team of berries comes together to create a magical potion that will keep you at the peak of health! Berries are full of antioxidants that keep free radicals from causing unwanted health problems, like vision loss and cancer, and there are plenty of berries to choose from when making this smoothie. Berries come in all shapes and colors too, so you can pick your favorite from the bunch. Try the red heart-shaped strawberry, the dark purple blackberry, the little blueberry, the exotic huckleberry, the tart raspberry, the juicy boysenberry, or the red cranberry. This smoothie calls for 1½ cups of "mixed berries," so pick a combination of the ones you like best. It's your chance to go wild and add your own creativity to the recipe! If you're unsure about what to choose, try a combination of blueberries, strawberries, and blackberries; this combination is a favorite. Mixing these berries with a generous portion of creamy canned coconut milk and a good splash of orange juice makes for a very indulging beverage. Sit back and enjoy your berry-tasting Paleo sips!

Time: 5 minutes | **Difficulty:** Easy | **Yields:** 20 ounces | **Serving size:** 10 ounces

1½ cups frozen mixed berries
1 cup orange juice, preferably freshly squeezed
1 cup canned coconut milk, chilled overnight

Place all ingredients in blender and blend on high until smooth.

NUTRITIONAL INFORMATION (PER SERVING SIZE):

CALORIES:	CARBOHYDRATES:	PROTEIN:	FAT:	SODIUM:	FIBER:	SUGAR:
297.5 (kcal)	21.25 (g)	3.75 (g)	24.5 (g)	30 (mg)	9.5 (g)	24.2 (g)

Concord Grape Smoothie

Grapes are so sweet, crisp, fun, and easy to eat. Eat one, and before you know it, the whole bunch is gone! These little bundles of joy are great to add to salads, to your morning fruit mix, to make juice, to ferment, and especially to add to your blender to make this amazing Concord Grape Smoothie. This smoothie uses the darker purple Concord grapes, which add a distinguished sweetness to this recipe—and a ton of healthy benefits as well! Concord grapes contain antioxidant and anti-inflammatory molecules that allow for blood pressure and cholesterol regulation, and can also provide your body with anti-cancer benefits. It's definitely good to include these little grapes in your diet. They will come to your rescue!

Time: 5 minutes | **Difficulty:** Easy | **Yields:** 20 ounces | **Serving size:** 10 ounces

1½ cups frozen seedless Concord grapes
1 frozen banana
1½ cups unsweetened vanilla almond milk

Place all ingredients in blender and blend on high until smooth.

NUTRITIONAL INFORMATION (PER SERVING SIZE):

CALORIES:	CARBOHYDRATES:	PROTEIN:	FAT:	SODIUM:	FIBER:	SUGAR:
160.5 (kcal)	36 (g)	2 (g)	2.25 (g)	274 (mg)	6 (g)	48.5 (g)

Green Smoothies

Green smoothies are drinks that blend leafy vegetables such as kale, spinach, lettuce, swiss chard, and celery with other all-natural ingredients such as fruits, herbs, nuts, seeds, and healthy oils. You can't help but smile when drinking the green smoothies found in this section. It might be because you know how good they are for you—you might as well be drinking an elixir of life—and because they're so unbelievably delicious! When making these smoothies, you should feel free to have fun and get really creative. The key to a good green smoothie is choosing one or two green ingredients, such as kale or spinach, and adding in a fun assortment of complementary fruits, liquids, and healthy fats, such as Paleo-approved oils or your favorite kind of nut. Green smoothies are a fantastic lunch or dinner replacement as they contain a plethora of nutrients that help feed your everyday mineral and vitamin needs. A green smoothie is always a fantastic meal option that is quick to make and one that will keep you focused and strong for the rest of the day. So whether you're drinking a Kale Power Smoothie, a Dandelion Greens Smoothie, or a Goji Good Smoothie, you know that you're harnessing the delicious power of good health!

Peachy Green Smoothie

This amazing Peachy Green Smoothie features some of the best natural flavors out there. The recipe calls for the incomparable taste of unfiltered apple juice, the unparalleled sweetness of raw honey, the catchy zing of freshly ground ginger, the freshness of coconut water, and the great combination of tartness and sweetness that comes from ripe peaches. In addition, this recipe calls for cashew butter to create a very creamy and smooth consistency. But cashew butter does more than just make this Paleo smoothie creamy; it actually helps keep your bones healthy, regulates your blood pressure, stabilizes your blood sugar, and keeps your muscles healthy. Cashew butter is a high-calorie food, so you don't want to go too crazy with it; however, do enjoy every tablespoon that this recipe calls for, and savor it with every sip!

Time: 5 minutes | **Difficulty:** Easy | **Yields:** 20 ounces | **Serving size:** 10 ounces

2 cups frozen peaches
2 cups baby spinach
1 cup organic unfiltered apple juice
2 tablespoons raw honey
2 tablespoons cashew butter
⅛ teaspoon ground ginger
3 coconut water ice cubes

Place all ingredients in blender and blend on high until smooth.

NUTRITIONAL INFORMATION (PER SERVING SIZE):

CALORIES:	CARBOHYDRATES:	PROTEIN:	FAT:	SODIUM:	FIBER:	SUGAR:
306.88 (kcal)	46.85 (g)	5.5 (g)	8 (g)	97.2 (mg)	7.5 (g)	70 (g)

Strawberry Mint Smoothie

Drinking this smoothie is just like taking a deep breath of fresh air. You'll get a sense of rejuvenation, empowerment, and energy afterward; what a wonderful feeling! Don't you wish you felt like this more often? Well, with the help of this creative fruity mixture, you can! Not only is this Paleo smoothie tremendously fresh, it's also tremendously—and naturally—sweet. The bananas, strawberries, and honey create this smoothie's sweetness, while the kale, coconut water, and mint help bring some balance to the mix. So sit back, take a deep breath, and relax with this refreshing green smoothie!

Time: 5 minutes | **Difficulty:** Easy | **Yields:** 20 ounces | **Serving size:** 10 ounces

1 frozen banana
1 cup frozen strawberries
1 cup baby kale
1½ cups coconut water
1 tablespoon raw honey
5 fresh mint leaves

Place all ingredients in blender and blend on high until smooth.

NUTRITIONAL INFORMATION (PER SERVING SIZE):

CALORIES:	CARBOHYDRATES:	PROTEIN:	FAT:	SODIUM:	FIBER:	SUGAR:
160 (kcal)	37.7 (g)	3.5 (g)	0 (g)	87 (mg)	11.5 (g)	47.5 (g)

Goji Good Smoothie

This smoothie is super delicious and good for you, and a big part of it has to do with the goji berry! In China, this little berry has been consumed by generations to help treat problems such as diabetes, fevers, high blood pressure, and vision decay. Furthermore, goji berries are are great for your mental health, help put you in a better mood, help improve sleep and athletic performance, and give you an overall sense of tranquility. While this Paleo smoothie uses fresh goji berries, this fruit can also be enjoyed cooked, dried, and blended. This smoothie not only hits the spot and calms your cravings, it also strengthens your system and keeps you living healthy. It seems like goji berries are the way to go, so take a sip and enjoy!

Time: 5 minutes | **Difficulty:** Easy | **Yields:** 24 ounces | **Serving size:** 8 ounces

½ cup frozen blueberries
1 frozen banana
¼ cup goji berries
1 cup baby spinach
1½ cups coconut water
2 tablespoons raw honey
1 teaspoon coconut butter

Place all ingredients in blender and blend on high until smooth.

NUTRITIONAL INFORMATION (PER SERVING SIZE):

CALORIES:	CARBOHYDRATES:	PROTEIN:	FAT:	SODIUM:	FIBER:	SUGAR:
199.1 (kcal)	43.8 (g)	12.7 (g)	0.8 (g)	293.5 (mg)	15.5 (g)	98 (g)

Green Fruit Smoothie

The color green symbolizes vigor, health, and life. Naturally green things are organisms that are healthy, strong, and working optimally. A green smoothie is exactly that: It's a drink full of goodness and health that can revive you and provide you with all you need to reach a state of ideal health and strength. Start your journey to good health with this delectable smoothie. Here, even some of the required fruits are green, which make for a very vibrant green drink. The spinach, coconut oil, green apple, banana, flaxseed, and honey will serve as a fantastic pick-me-up in your day and will completely revive you if you're in a slump. So drink your greens and stay on top of your game!

Time: 5 minutes | **Difficulty:** Easy | **Yields:** 20 ounces | **Serving size:** 10 ounces

½ cup frozen seedless green grapes
1 frozen banana
1 green apple, cored
1 cup spinach
1½ cups coconut water
1 teaspoon coconut oil
2 tablespoons raw honey
1 teaspoon flaxseed

Place all ingredients in blender and blend on high until smooth.

NUTRITIONAL INFORMATION (PER SERVING SIZE):

CALORIES:	CARBOHYDRATES:	PROTEIN:	FAT:	SODIUM:	FIBER:	SUGAR:
244.65 (kcal)	55.35 (g)	2.75 (g)	2.85 (g)	84.2 (mg)	13 (g)	84.5 (g)

Dandelion Greens Smoothie

This smoothie will make you feel like you're in the middle of a secret garden, surrounded by wonderful herbs, plants, and flowers. It's soothing and satisfying, just like a good green smoothie should be. Dandelion greens tend to have a mild bitter flavor to them, but when prepared properly or combined with the right ingredients—like the neutralizing chamomile herb—its flavor can really add to the taste of your smoothie. In addition, dandelion greens are packed with calcium, vitamin A, and vitamin K. They also promote urine production that can help you reduce severe liver, gallbladder, and kidney issues. Go dandelions!

Time: 5 minutes | **Difficulty:** Easy | **Yields:** 20 ounces | **Serving size:** 10 ounces

1 frozen banana
½ cup frozen raspberries
½ avocado
1 cup dandelion greens
1½ cups freshly made iced chamomile tea
Juice of ½ lemon
2 tablespoons raw honey
½ teaspoon chia seeds

Place all ingredients in blender and blend on high until smooth.

NUTRITIONAL INFORMATION (PER SERVING SIZE):

CALORIES:	CARBOHYDRATES:	PROTEIN:	FAT:	SODIUM:	FIBER:	SUGAR:
234.2 (kcal)	42.5 (g)	2.43 (g)	8 (g)	53.4 (mg)	16.4 (g)	52.5 (g)

Spiced Pear Smoothie

Pears and spice create a wondrous autumn combination that will awaken your senses and add some flavor to your life. This green smoothie has just the right balance of sweet and tart, which makes it really easy to drink, and it contains some great greens like arugula and kale that will nourish your body by providing lots of great fiber and iron. In addition, this recipe calls for some sassy cayenne pepper to bring this Paleo smoothie to the next level! Just a small pinch of this spice helps accentuate all the flavors in this smoothie. This little spice has been widely used around the world to help soothe a plethora of ailments including headache, allergies, fevers, hemorrhoids, nausea, tonsillitis, sore throats, and delirium. So get ready to enjoy the zesty kick of this Spiced Pear Smoothie!

Time: 5 minutes | **Difficulty:** Easy | **Yields:** 20 ounces | **Serving size:** 10 ounces

1½ frozen bananas
1 ripe pear, cored
½ cup kale
½ cup arugula
1 cup coconut water
⅛ teaspoon cayenne pepper
¼ teaspoon cinnamon
⅛ teaspoon ground ginger

Place all ingredients in blender and blend on high until smooth.

NUTRITIONAL INFORMATION (PER SERVING SIZE):

CALORIES:	CARBOHYDRATES:	PROTEIN:	FAT:	SODIUM:	FIBER:	SUGAR:
155.1 (kcal)	58.6 (g)	3.5 (g)	0 (g)	273.7 (mg)	17.75 (g)	63 (g)

Greens with a Kick Smoothie

Are you ready for a green smoothie with a kick? This Greens with a Kick Smoothie is made to order! The chili powder adds a spicy note to this smoothie, but it doesn't overpower the other ingredients; if anything, mixing it with avocado, blueberries, coconut, kale, and cinnamon only make each of these ingredients shine brighter! In addition to being spicy and delicious, this Paleo smoothie is a great meal replacement; the healthy fats from the avocado, the great nutrients from the kale, the antioxidants and vitamins from the blueberries, and the wonderful carbohydrates from the coconut and honey will keep you going strong. Blend this array of colors and flavors, pour it into a large mug, kick back, and enjoy this full-of-spice pick-me-up!

Time: 5 minutes | **Difficulty:** Easy | **Yields:** 16 ounces | **Serving size:** 8 ounces

1½ cups frozen blueberries
½ avocado
1 cup kale
1 cup coconut water
2 tablespoons raw honey
1 teaspoon coconut cream concentrate
⅛ teaspoon chili powder
¼ teaspoon cinnamon
3 coconut water ice cubes

Place all ingredients in blender and blend on high until smooth.

NUTRITIONAL INFORMATION (PER SERVING SIZE):

CALORIES:	CARBOHYDRATES:	PROTEIN:	FAT:	SODIUM:	FIBER:	SUGAR:
276.25 (kcal)	48.05 (g)	5.75 (g)	9 (g)	315.1 (mg)	18.35 (g)	68 (g)

Rosemary Mint Smoothie

The combination of rosemary and mint creates a marvelous culinary experience, and that's exactly what you find in this Paleo Rosemary Mint Smoothie. When mixed with strawberries and honey, the fresh herbs guarantee smoothie success. This green smoothie is a really nice spring drink. It awakens your senses and reminds you of those bright mornings when the grass is green and the flowers are blooming, so give it a try on those days when you need a little pick-me-up. In addition to freshening up your day, the nutrients in the rosemary can have a physical effect on you. This herb has been shown to have a positive effect on your brain, as it contains carnosic acid that helps you fight free radical damages. Also, some oils found in rosemary have been proven to help improve concentration and enhance memory. What a great little herb—and what an amazing green smoothie!

Time: 5 minutes | **Difficulty:** Easy | **Yields:** 20 ounces | **Serving size:** 10 ounces

1 cup frozen strawberries
1 frozen banana
2 cups baby spinach
1½ cups coconut water
2 tablespoons chopped rosemary leaves
3 fresh mint leaves
2 tablespoons raw honey

Place all ingredients in blender and blend on high until smooth.

NUTRITIONAL INFORMATION (PER SERVING SIZE):

CALORIES:	CARBOHYDRATES:	PROTEIN:	FAT:	SODIUM:	FIBER:	SUGAR:
184.5 (kcal)	44.2 (g)	3.5 (g)	0 (g)	107 (mg)	12.5 (g)	65 (g)

Kale Power Smoothie

Can you feel the power of kale? If not, you will after you drink this Kale Power Smoothie! Kale is a super-healthy green full of nutrients that can help you in many ways. It is high in iron, which encourages better liver function and cell growth in your body and helps your body detox. It also has great amounts of vitamin K, which protects against cancer and other diseases; is an anti-inflammatory and antioxidant food that aids those with problems like arthritis and asthma; helps lower cholesterol; and can even improve your skin and vision. Kale rocks! Kale—especially baby kale, which has a smoother taste—is also really easy to add to your smoothies. In fact, when you blend it in with fruits, nuts, spices, and natural sweeteners, you can get away with using lots of kale because you won't even taste it. Go ahead and try this yummy smoothie. You're sure to feel its health power after you sip it down!

Time: 5 minutes | **Difficulty:** Easy | **Yields:** 20 ounces | **Serving size:** 10 ounces

1 frozen banana
½ cup frozen blackberries
2 cups baby kale
1½ cups unsweetened almond milk
1 tablespoon raw honey
¼ teaspoon cinnamon
1 tablespoon coconut oil

Place all ingredients in blender and blend on high until smooth.

NUTRITIONAL INFORMATION (PER SERVING SIZE):

CALORIES:	CARBOHYDRATES:	PROTEIN:	FAT:	SODIUM:	FIBER:	SUGAR:
221.75 (kcal)	34 (g)	3.75 (g)	9.5 (g)	330.5 (mg)	10.75 (g)	35 (g)

Greens Galore Smoothie

Did you know that romaine lettuce contains all eight essential amino acids that make a complete protein, and that one head of romaine lettuce has 7.7 grams of protein? This green also has more vitamin C than an orange! One head of romaine lettuce has 167 percent of the required daily intake, while an orange only has 92 percent. Crazy good, right? This leafy ingredient keeps your digestive system healthy with all of its fiber, lowers high blood pressure with its potassium, reduces the risk of heart attacks with its folic acid, and keeps your immune system in check with its vitamins A, B_1, B_2, C, and K. Get excited for this Paleo smoothie. It's going to do your body good!

Time: 5 minutes | **Difficulty:** Easy | **Yields:** 24 ounces | **Serving size:** 8 ounces

1½ frozen bananas
1 green apple, cored
1 green pear, cored
½ cup baby spinach
½ cup baby kale
½ cup romaine lettuce
1½ cups coconut water
2 Medjool dates, pitted
1 teaspoon lime juice, preferably freshly squeezed

Place all ingredients in blender and blend on high until smooth.

NUTRITIONAL INFORMATION (PER SERVING SIZE):

CALORIES:	CARBOHYDRATES:	PROTEIN:	FAT:	SODIUM:	FIBER:	SUGAR:
185.2 (kcal)	60.47 (g)	3.3 (g)	0 (g)	89.75 (mg)	27.5 (g)	114.75 (g)

Prickly Pear Green Smoothie

This is one of those smoothies you will have lots of fun making. Why? Because of its use of a super-delicious and exotic ingredient, the prickly pear! Widely available in Ecuador, prickly pears have a very unique taste that is quite sweet and very unlike any other fruit. You can eat them by themselves, add them to a salad, or use them in your Prickly Pear Green Smoothie! This delicious cactus-like fruit is packed full of fiber to aid digestion; potassium and magnesium to help balance fluids in your body and regulate blood pressure; vitamin A to improve your skin and vision; and lots of vitamin C to boost your immune system. Give this little exotic gem of a smoothie a try, and introduce the great prickly pear to your Paleo diet if you haven't already!

Time: 5 minutes | **Difficulty:** Easy | **Yields:** 16 ounces | **Serving size:** 8 ounces

Juice of 1 prickly pear
Juice of ½ cucumber
Juice of 1 celery stalk
1 cup frozen pineapple chunks
1 red apple, cored
1 cup kale
Juice of 1 lemon
2 tablespoons raw honey
3 coconut water ice cubes

1. Place the prickly pear, cucumber, and celery stalk in a juicer and follow its instructions. Use the juice only and discard the pulp.
2. Place all ingredients in blender and blend on high until smooth.

NUTRITIONAL INFORMATION (PER SERVING SIZE):

CALORIES:	CARBOHYDRATES:	PROTEIN:	FAT:	SODIUM:	FIBER:	SUGAR:
212.25 (kcal)	52.9 (g)	2.74 (g)	0.5 (g)	113 (mg)	13.3 (g)	71.4 (g)

Basily Good Smoothie

Have you ever gotten close to a fresh basil plant in summer and smelled its leaves? It's one of the best and purest fragrances you will ever have the pleasure of smelling. And that's just the beginning! Basil not only exudes an amazing aroma, it adds incredible flavor to recipes. In this Basily Good Smoothie, the combination of strawberries, oranges, greens, and this fantastic herb will delight your taste buds. The smoothie will feel fresh, sweet, and tangy, and it's an ideal drink for hot summer days or after a nice long run. Enjoy.

Time: 5 minutes | **Difficulty:** Easy | **Yields:** 20 ounces | **Serving size:** 10 ounces

1½ cups frozen strawberries
2 cups baby spinach
2 cups orange juice, preferably freshly squeezed
⅛ cup fresh basil

Place all ingredients in blender and blend on high until smooth.

NUTRITIONAL INFORMATION (PER SERVING SIZE):

CALORIES:	CARBOHYDRATES:	PROTEIN:	FAT:	SODIUM:	FIBER:	SUGAR:
89.5 (kcal)	21 (g)	2.75 (g)	0 (g)	51 (mg)	10.5 (g)	28.5 (g)

Orchard Green Smoothie

You may think that you'd rather drink a smoothie packed full of sweet fruits or savory vegetables than one full of spinach and kale, but this Orchard Green Smoothie gives you the best of both worlds! It's very important to eat enough greens; and the nutrients spinach and kale bring to this Paleo smoothie are beyond measure. Kale has more vitamin C than oranges, it contains omega-3 fatty acids, it is packed with vitamin A, and it has more calcium than milk. Amazing, right? Spinach has a plethora of minerals; provides you with vitamins A, K, D, and E; and contains antioxidants that help combat inflammation and diseases. One cup of this fantastic green gives you 200 percent of your daily value for vitamin K, which helps keep your bones strong. So take a sip and enjoy the combination of these two greens along with tasty oranges, strawberries, ginger, and lemons. It's a green party in a glass!

Time: 5 minutes | **Difficulty:** Easy | **Yields:** 16 ounces | **Serving size:** 8 ounces

Juice of 6 carrots
1 cup frozen strawberries
2 seedless oranges, peeled
½ cup baby spinach
½ cup baby kale
Juice ½ lemon
¼ teaspoon freshly grated ginger

1. Place carrots in a juicer and follow its instructions. Use the juice only and discard the pulp.
2. Place all ingredients in blender and blend on high until smooth.

NUTRITIONAL INFORMATION (PER SERVING SIZE):

CALORIES:	CARBOHYDRATES:	PROTEIN:	FAT:	SODIUM:	FIBER:	SUGAR:
129.75 (kcal)	31 (g)	3.25 (g)	0 (g)	96.5 (mg)	10 (g)	34.5 (g)

Smooth Beets Smoothie

Yum, doesn't thinking about how smooth, bright red, soft, and sweet beets are make you want to eat them right now? Many people do not eat beets on a regular basis, but they should. Beets not only add so much flavor and color to your foods, they also help you live a better life. Beets have multiple health benefits, but one of the greatest is that they work in the liver to help cleanse your blood and help prevent you from getting various diseases such as cancer. Beets also have a higher sugar content than other root vegetables, and can give you a great source of energy when you need an extra push to get through the day. Beets can also help prevent tumor formations, and they are beneficial to your eye health. They help strengthen your hair, reduce skin imperfections, promote liver health, and normalize blood pressure. So drink up! This Paleo Smooth Beets Smoothie will satiate your sweet cravings and keep you extra healthy!

Time: 5 minutes | **Difficulty:** Easy | **Yields:** 20 ounces | **Serving size:** 10 ounces

Juice of 1 beet
1½ cups frozen pineapple chunks
1 frozen banana
1 cup baby spinach
1 cup coconut water
Juice of ½ lemon

1. Place beet in a juicer and follow its instructions. Use the juice only and discard the pulp.
2. Place all ingredients in blender and blend on high until smooth.

NUTRITIONAL INFORMATION (PER SERVING SIZE):

CALORIES:	CARBOHYDRATES:	PROTEIN:	FAT:	SODIUM:	FIBER:	SUGAR:
177.5 (kcal)	43 (g)	4.25 (g)	0 (g)	568 (mg)	14 (g)	54.5 (g)

Green Strength Smoothie

Spinach was Popeye's ingredient of choice for a good reason. This green, leafy vegetable is one of the most nutritious foods you can eat. One cup of spinach is only 40 calories, contains more vitamin A and vitamin K than the required daily amounts, and provides your body with multiple nutrients such as calcium, protein, and fiber. Spinach can help fight prostate and ovarian cancers, and it improves brain function and cardiovascular health. In addition, spinach helps give green smoothies a creamier consistency when compared to any other leafy vegetable because it blends very well and breaks down completely. It also has a very light taste that does not compete with other ingredients, making it a really easy ingredient to combine with other vegetables and fruits.

Time: 5 minutes | **Difficulty:** Easy | **Yields:** 20 ounces | **Serving size:** 10 ounces

1 frozen banana
½ cup frozen strawberries
2 cups spinach
1 cup organic unfiltered apple juice
½ cup coconut water
1 teaspoon spirulina

Place all ingredients in blender and blend on high until smooth.

NUTRITIONAL INFORMATION (PER SERVING SIZE):

CALORIES:	CARBOHYDRATES:	PROTEIN:	FAT:	SODIUM:	FIBER:	SUGAR:
158 (kcal)	27.75 (g)	3.25 (g)	0.25 (g)	129.5 (mg)	8 (g)	50.5 (g)

Fruits-Only Smoothies

Have you ever gone a little overboard at the grocery store and bought more bananas or apples than you would ever be able to eat? Now, instead of throwing that beautiful produce into the trash when it goes bad, all you have to do is freeze your fruit and keep it handy for some tasty Fruits-Only Smoothies. Just picture a freezer full of peaches, bananas, berries, mangos, and pineapples that you can turn to any time you're looking for ingredients to curb those Paleo cravings. Fruits keep really well in the freezer and stay in a perfect smoothie condition by the time a nice drink is needed. In this section, you'll find a bunch of fruit-only smoothies like the Piña Colada Smoothie, the Guava Fruit Smoothie, and the Strawberry Mandarin Smoothie that are so delicious, they'll leave you wanting more! If you're putting together your own fruit-only smoothie, feel free to grab any random ingredients—both fresh and frozen—that you have at your disposal. You'll be pleasantly surprised with all the great combinations you discover. Bottoms up!

Summertime Smoothie

Don't you love how happy, energized, excited, and adventurous summer always makes you feel? Get that summer feeling any time of the year with this Summertime Smoothie! The mangos, banana, and strawberries combine to create a drink that is just as fresh as those glorious early summer mornings, but the freshness of the spearmint tea is a unique twist that bumps this Paleo smoothie to the next level. In addition to being delicious, this tea is really healthy, too. Among some of its benefits, caffeine-free spearmint is said to make you more alert, keep you calm and centered, and even reduce unwanted hair in women! Furthermore, spearmint is fabulous for your digestive tract, relieving stomachaches, abdominal pain, indigestion, nausea, and heartburn. Spearmint can also help you get through a cold by decongesting your sinuses, clearing your nasal passages, and reducing throat soreness with its anti-inflammatory properties. This fresh little leaf has so much to offer, and nothing is better than feeling its freshness packed into this Summertime Smoothie!

Time: 5 minutes | **Difficulty:** Easy | **Yields:** 20 ounces | **Serving size:** 10 ounces

1½ cups frozen mango slices
1 frozen banana
1 cup ripe strawberries
1 cup freshly made iced organic spearmint tea

Place all ingredients in blender and blend on high until smooth.

NUTRITIONAL INFORMATION (PER SERVING SIZE):

CALORIES:	CARBOHYDRATES:	PROTEIN:	FAT:	SODIUM:	FIBER:	SUGAR:
156.5 (kcal)	40.5 (g)	1.75 (g)	0 (g)	7.5 (mg)	10.5 (g)	57 (g)

Pineapple Paradise Smoothie

Let flavor transport you to a place of wonder! Just close your eyes and let this Pineapple Paradise Smoothie take you to a magical place where palm trees grow tall, seagulls fly, and the sun shines bright. This is a place where you can go when all things in life accumulate and seem to be out of your control. It can be a place that brings solace and comfort. This smoothie will not only provide you with a wonderful mental break, but it will also feed your body right. The ingredients in this fruit smoothie reduce pain and inflammation, prevent colds, improve nutrient absorption, help you maintain healthy circulation, strengthen your immune system, keep your bones strong and skin beautiful, and more! Take care of your health and proactively fuel your body with this Paleo smoothie. You're guaranteed to feel like you're in paradise!

Time: 5 minutes | **Difficulty:** Easy | **Yields:** 20 ounces | **Serving size:** 10 ounces

1½ cups frozen pineapple chunks
1 frozen banana
1½ cups orange juice, preferably freshly squeezed
½ teaspoon freshly grated ginger

Place all ingredients in blender and blend on high until smooth.

NUTRITIONAL INFORMATION (PER SERVING SIZE):

CALORIES:	CARBOHYDRATES:	PROTEIN:	FAT:	SODIUM:	FIBER:	SUGAR:
198.5 (kcal)	49.5 (g)	2 (g)	0 (g)	7 (mg)	6 (g)	69.5 (g)

Classic Strawberry Smoothie

Strawberry is to a smoothie like Hershey's is to chocolate. They're classics! Strawberries are widely used for smoothies around the world because they bring a sweet taste, a nice consistency, a nice look, and a wonderful array of health benefits. Another great thing about this sweet fruit is that it's very low in calories, so you can add as many strawberries to a smoothie as you'd like and still keep the calorie count fairly low. The fruit also blends really well with other fruits, which also makes it an ideal smoothie ingredient. These little pink bursts of flavor are superhero fruits that provide you with magnificent benefits. You'll love this one!

Time: 5 minutes | **Difficulty:** Easy | **Yields:** 20 ounces | **Serving size:** 10 ounces

1 frozen banana
1 cup frozen strawberries
1½ cups orange juice, preferably freshly squeezed

Place all ingredients in blender and blend on high until smooth.

NUTRITIONAL INFORMATION (PER SERVING SIZE):

CALORIES:	CARBOHYDRATES:	PROTEIN:	FAT:	SODIUM:	FIBER:	SUGAR:
161 (kcal)	39 (g)	1.75 (g)	0 (g)	6 (mg)	6 (g)	52.5 (g)

Fruits Rule Smoothie

Let's be honest about it: Fruits rule. You can do so much with them: You can eat them as-is, add them to salads, make amazing juices and desserts with them, create jams with them, use them for coloring . . . the possibilities are truly endless. This super, natural-tasting smoothie is packed with some serious pure, sweet, fresh, juicy flavor, thanks to some of your favorite fruits. You might want to drink this Paleo Fruits Rule Smoothie to curb any cravings or to satisfy your sweet tooth. What are you waiting for? It's time to whip up this smoothie and never look back!

Time: 5 minutes | **Difficulty:** Easy | **Yields:** 16 ounces | **Serving size:** 8 ounces

½ **cup frozen mango slices**
½ **cup frozen raspberries**
½ **cup frozen strawberries**
½ **cup pineapple chunks**
1 cup organic pineapple juice

Place all ingredients in blender and blend on high until smooth.

NUTRITIONAL INFORMATION (PER SERVING SIZE):

CALORIES:	CARBOHYDRATES:	PROTEIN:	FAT:	SODIUM:	FIBER:	SUGAR:
141.25 (kcal)	35.25 (g)	1.5 (g)	0.25 (g)	9 (mg)	8 (g)	51 (g)

It's All Yellow Smoothie

Yellow is in! Yellow is great! Yellow shouts out "happy!" In this delicious, fruit-filled smoothie, you'll find three gorgeous types of yellow fruits: bananas, pineapples, and mangos. This yellow-full smoothie will make you bounce with joy, not only because of how pretty it looks, but also because of its delicious taste and its wonderful nutritional content. This full-of-goodness yellow smoothie will provide you with high levels of potassium, which help you with proper muscle and nerve function; vitamins A, B_1, B_6, C, and E, which are great immune system boosters and serve as antioxidant defenders; lots of fiber to help you digest your foods properly; and great complex carbohydrates that are a fantastic source of energy. Enjoy this taste of "happy," and go shine as bright as the big yellow sun!

Time: 5 minutes | **Difficulty:** Easy | **Yields:** 20 ounces | **Serving size:** 10 ounces

2 frozen bananas
2 cups pineapple chunks
2 cups ripe mango slices

Place all ingredients in blender and blend on high until smooth.

NUTRITIONAL INFORMATION (PER SERVING SIZE):

CALORIES:	CARBOHYDRATES:	PROTEIN:	FAT:	SODIUM:	FIBER:	SUGAR:
294 (kcal)	77 (g)	3 (g)	0 (g)	12 (mg)	16 (g)	108 (g)

Peach Perfect Smoothie

The *Merriam-Webster Dictionary* describes the word "perfect" as "being entirely without fault of defect," and *perfect* is exactly what this Peach Perfect Smoothie is! The sweet peaches combine with juicy strawberries, creamy bananas, and tangy tangerines to make a perfect punch of flavor. You can use either white or yellow peaches in this fruity Paleo smoothie. Whichever one you pick will go fabulously with the other smoothie ingredients and will have your taste buds buzzing with perfection all day long. Enjoy perfection!

Time: 5 minutes | **Difficulty:** Easy | **Yields:** 20 ounces | **Serving size:** 10 ounces

1 cup frozen strawberries
1 frozen banana
2 ripe peaches, cored
4 seedless tangerines, peeled
1 cup coconut water

Place all ingredients in blender and blend on high until smooth.

NUTRITIONAL INFORMATION (PER SERVING SIZE):

CALORIES:	CARBOHYDRATES:	PROTEIN:	FAT:	SODIUM:	FIBER:	SUGAR:
240 (kcal)	59 (g)	5 (g)	0 (g)	263 (mg)	17 (g)	61 (g)

Very Berry Good Smoothie

Did you know that after strawberries, blueberries are the most popular berries consumed in the United States? Even though blueberries are small fruits, they are considered a superfood because they contain high levels of fiber, manganese, phytonutrients, and vitamin C. This juicy, colorful, and plump fruit is also packed with fantastic antioxidants that help your body fight against free radicals. Recent studies have shown that blueberries help keep your brain and nervous system healthy, reduce the risk of cancer, and also improve memory when consumed on a daily basis. Go blueberries!

Time: 5 minutes | **Difficulty:** Easy | **Yields:** 20 ounces | **Serving size:** 10 ounces

1 frozen banana
1 cup frozen blueberries
1½ cup organic unfiltered apple juice
½ cup coconut water
1 tablespoon unsweetened shredded coconut

Place all ingredients in blender and blend on high until smooth.

NUTRITIONAL INFORMATION (PER SERVING SIZE):

CALORIES:	CARBOHYDRATES:	PROTEIN:	FAT:	SODIUM:	FIBER:	SUGAR:
227.5 (kcal)	38.15 (g)	1.65 (g)	1.65 (g)	59.2 (mg)	9.2 (g)	77.3 (g)

Piña Colada Smoothie

Oh, the wonderful taste of piña coladas. All it takes is a sip to transport you to a warm paradise where you can almost hear the ocean, feel the breeze, and smell the salt in the air. What is it about this Paleo smoothie that takes you to a place where you can feel the soft touch of sand on your feet and breathe in the soft ocean air? The coconut milk, of course! One of the best attributes of the coconut milk used in this recipe is that it's very creamy, which makes this smoothie very much like the thick piña coladas delivered to you as you lounge in a cabana. Also, canned coconut milk's pronounced coconut taste adds a lot to the overall smoothie flavor, making it extra sweet and tropical-tasting. So whip up this fruit-filled smoothie, enjoy a nice splash of sunshine on your skin, close your eyes, take a sip, and let your sense of taste take you to the beach!

Time: 5 minutes | **Difficulty:** Easy | **Yields:** 16 ounces | **Serving size:** 8 ounces

1 frozen banana
1 cup frozen pineapple chunks
1 cup organic pineapple juice
⅓ cup canned coconut milk, chilled overnight

Place all ingredients in blender and blend on high until smooth.

NUTRITIONAL INFORMATION (PER SERVING SIZE):

CALORIES:	CARBOHYDRATES:	PROTEIN:	FAT:	SODIUM:	FIBER:	SUGAR:
233.65 (kcal)	41.5 (g)	2.35 (g)	8 (g)	17.7 (mg)	5 (g)	55 (g)

Passion Time Smoothie

Being passionate means emotionally connecting with something and having a strong drive to fulfill certain responsibilities to the best of your ability. If you consider yourself a person full of passion, then this Paleo smoothie fits right into your lifestyle! This little gem is full of bold fruit flavors and rich colors, matched with a nice smooth consistency. The tangy passion fruit added to the mix will give you vitamins that aid your vision, help cleanse your system, keep your heart healthy, and allow you to get better sleep. The mango, bananas, and coconut will give you lots of great fiber to help digestion and help improve your immune system. Drink this Passion Time Smoothie with passion, and let it help you fuel your passion for life!

Time: 5 minutes | **Difficulty:** Easy | **Yields:** 20 ounces | **Serving size:** 10 ounces

1½ frozen bananas
1 cup frozen mango slices
½ cup passion fruit
1½ cups coconut water

Place all ingredients in blender and blend on high until smooth.

NUTRITIONAL INFORMATION (PER SERVING SIZE):

CALORIES:	CARBOHYDRATES:	PROTEIN:	FAT:	SODIUM:	FIBER:	SUGAR:
224 (kcal)	74.95 (g)	4.75 (g)	0.5 (g)	93 (mg)	29 (g)	88 (g)

Guava Fruit Smoothie

There are some days when you feel a little frisky; when you feel extra vibrant and look dashing; and "extraordinary" becomes a part of your persona. On those days, you need to find a treat to match your fun personality and to sustain your great energy. Fortunately, this Guava Fruit Smoothie will give you all you need to make your day a playful one. The delicious combination of guava and strawberries, the tropical blend of mangos and coconut, and the added hint of sweet bananas will delight your taste buds and make you want to shout with glee. This fruity smoothie is not only extremely tasty, it is also very nutritious. It has lots of fiber, vitamins, and potassium to keep your bones healthy and your immune system strong. Drinking this fruit-filled Paleo treat is one of the best things you can do to show your body appreciation for all the things it does. Cheers to life—and to having more guava smoothies!

Time: 5 minutes | **Difficulty:** Easy | **Yields:** 20 ounces | **Serving size:** 10 ounces

1 frozen banana
½ cup frozen strawberries
½ cup frozen mango slices
1 cup ripe guava flesh
1½ cups coconut water
1 teaspoon unsweetened shredded coconut (to garnish)

1. Place all ingredients in blender, except for the shredded coconut, and blend on high until smooth.
2. Pour smoothie in glass and garnish with half of the shredded coconut. Enjoy!

NUTRITIONAL INFORMATION (PER SERVING SIZE):

CALORIES:	CARBOHYDRATES:	PROTEIN:	FAT:	SODIUM:	FIBER:	SUGAR:
189.75 (kcal)	42.5 (g)	4.58 (g)	1.8 (g)	61.3 (mg)	19.85 (g)	53.65 (g)

Tropical Grape Smoothie

The sweet coconut flavor and smooth texture of this smoothie will take you on a wonderful journey to the tropics and help you become healthier! If you haven't tried coconut cream concentrate, the main ingredient in this Paleo smoothie, you're in for a treat. Coconut cream concentrate is basically coconut meat in concentrated form. It is an all-natural ingredient that is made from finely grinding the coconut, and its creamy, nut-butter consistency comes from the high concentration of healthy fats that coconut meat contains. Coconut cream concentrate doesn't have any water in it, which means that it has not been diluted and retains all the nutrients and fiber that comes from coconut meat. Because of its buttery feel, some people refer to this ingredient as coconut butter. So choose today as the day that you become healthier and feel extra amazing. This tropical grape delight will get you there!

Time: 5 minutes | **Difficulty:** Easy | **Yields:** 16 ounces | **Serving size:** 8 ounces

1½ cups frozen seedless red grapes
1 frozen banana
1 cup ripe strawberries
1 teaspoon coconut cream concentrate
1 cup coconut water

Place all ingredients in blender and blend on high until smooth.

NUTRITIONAL INFORMATION (PER SERVING SIZE):

CALORIES:	CARBOHYDRATES:	PROTEIN:	FAT:	SODIUM:	FIBER:	SUGAR:
188.5 (kcal)	45.5 (g)	4.25 (g)	1.5 (g)	44 (mg)	10.5 (g)	62.5 (g)

Avocado O'Clock Smoothie

It's time for the creamy, smooth, and very green avocado. Some people spread it on bread, some have it on salads, and some have it in guacamole, but using it in this Avocado O'Clock Smoothie puts those other methods to shame! Aside from making your smoothies extra smooth and velvety, avocados contain all the essential amino acids that your body needs to be able to form protein. The cool thing about this type of protein is that it is a lot easier for the body to digest than animal protein, as it also contains tons of fiber. Avocados also have fantastic healthy fats that increase the level of good cholesterol in your body, which helps to prevent diabetes. Furthermore, avocados are a rich source of carotenoids, which aid eye and reproductive health. Avocados are a great fruit; there's nothing like them, really. Don't you wish it was always avocado o'clock?

Time: 5 minutes | **Difficulty:** Easy | **Yields:** 20 ounces | **Serving size:** 10 ounces

1 cup frozen mango slices
1 frozen banana
½ avocado
1½ cups unsweetened coconut milk (from carton, not canned)
Juice of ½ lemon

Place all ingredients in blender and blend on high until smooth.

NUTRITIONAL INFORMATION (PER SERVING SIZE):

CALORIES:	CARBOHYDRATES:	PROTEIN:	FAT:	SODIUM:	FIBER:	SUGAR:
223.25 (kcal)	34.25 (g)	2 (g)	10.5 (g)	34 (mg)	14 (g)	40.5 (g)

Cheery Cherry Smoothie

Do you want to get cheery with cherries? Of course you do! After all, there is nothing like a sweet delight to make your day extra bright. The cherries in this Paleo smoothie give this drink a great punch of flavor, but they also feed your body and keep you strong and healthy. These bright, shiny red sweet cherries have a plethora of nutrients that are beneficial to your health and also contain antioxidants that are practically exclusive to this fruit. Cherries have anti-inflammatory properties that help with arthritis and sports injuries, and they're also rich in melatonin, an antioxidant that will help you turn around irritable moods, prevent insomnia, and soothe headaches. Beta-carotene, another important antioxidant, is also present in sweet cherries, and it works to protect you from harmful free radicals. With every sip you take of this smoothie, feel cheery and let cherries do their work. Find peace in knowing that all of these wonderful antioxidants will protect you and keep you safe. Go cherries!

Time: 5 minutes | **Difficulty:** Easy | **Yields:** 16 ounces | **Serving size:** 8 ounces

1½ cups frozen peach slices
½ cup frozen sweet cherries, pitted
1¼ cups unsweetened coconut milk (from carton, not canned)

Place all ingredients in blender and blend on high until smooth.

NUTRITIONAL INFORMATION (PER SERVING SIZE):

CALORIES:	CARBOHYDRATES:	PROTEIN:	FAT:	SODIUM:	FIBER:	SUGAR:
94.88 (kcal)	19 (g)	1 (g)	2.8 (g)	18.75 (mg)	5.75 (g)	11.75 (g)

Blue Lemon Smoothie

You may have heard that lemons are good for you, and that they have great beauty and cleansing benefits. But do you really know how amazing they are? Because of their citrusy composition, lemons have been proven to help you fight against infections. They can also help prevent cancer, cardiovascular diseases, and strokes; lower blood pressure and increase levels of good cholesterol; and can even give your skin a fantastic glow and make you look fresh. Lemon juice has also been proven to relieve tongue inflammation, stomatitis, and gingivitis; help prevent common colds; help relieve gastric issues and colic pain; and can help you prevent dehydration and osteoarthritis. Isn't it amazing how many benefits you can get just from one tiny fruit? Luckily, lemons are sold everywhere and are fairly inexpensive. Use this to your benefit and add this all-natural medicine to your diet.

Time: 5 minutes | **Difficulty:** Easy | **Yields:** 16 ounces | **Serving size:** 8 ounces

1 cup frozen blueberries
1 cup frozen white peach slices
1 cup coconut water
Juice of 1 lemon

Place all ingredients in blender and blend on high until smooth.

NUTRITIONAL INFORMATION (PER SERVING SIZE):

CALORIES:	CARBOHYDRATES:	PROTEIN:	FAT:	SODIUM:	FIBER:	SUGAR:
101 (kcal)	24.5 (g)	2 (g)	0 (g)	253 (mg)	9 (g)	23 (g)

Strawberry Mandarin Smoothie

Doesn't this Strawberry Mandarin Smoothie just sound wonderfully refreshing and thirst quenching? Well, it actually is! And the fruit that adds a lot to this smoothie is the cute little mandarin, also known as mandarin oranges or tangerines. Mandarins have been proven to reduce your risk of cancer and may help you lose weight. This delightful small fruit is also loaded with vitamin C, which boosts your metabolism and helps you fight infections, as well as a great amount of antioxidants that can help lower your cholesterol levels. Mandarins are a great fruit to eat as a snack by themselves, but they're even more delicious when mixed with complementary fruits like the strawberries, bananas, and oranges used in this Paleo recipe. Drink up and enjoy!

Time: 5 minutes | **Difficulty:** Easy | **Yields:** 16 ounces | **Serving size:** 8 ounces

1 frozen banana
1 cup frozen strawberries
3 seedless mandarins, peeled
1 cup orange juice, preferably freshly squeezed

Place all ingredients in blender and blend on high until smooth.

NUTRITIONAL INFORMATION (PER SERVING SIZE):

CALORIES:	CARBOHYDRATES:	PROTEIN:	FAT:	SODIUM:	FIBER:	SUGAR:
159.5 (kcal)	40 (g)	3 (g)	0 (g)	9 (mg)	11 (g)	54 (g)

Exotic Smoothies

There are so many crazy fruits around the planet that you may not usually come across in your grocery store's produce section. But if you open your mind—and your taste buds—you'll soon find yourself becoming bold, brave, wild, and even a little exotic! For the recipes in this section, like the Dragon Fruit Thrill Smoothie, the Blackberry Naranjilla Smoothie, and the Tomate de Árbol Smoothie, you'll use fruits that may sound and look extremely unusual; you may even be a little scared of some of the spikes on these exotic wonders! But throw caution to the wind and get your culinary adventure on. It's guaranteed to be a fun and delicious ride. Let your taste buds rejoice and explore a whole new world!

Mango Tango Smoothie

Want to tango with mango? This mango and passion fruit smoothie is one of those drinks that will make you want to get on your feet and dance your little heart out. It is smooth, citrusy, sweet, and full of zing. Just by smelling this mixture's fragrance, you'll discover the sweet taste that awaits you after you pour the smoothie in your favorite glass, add a straw, and take your first sip. Mangos are very rich in vitamins, minerals, prebiotic dietary fiber, and antioxidants, and the very delicious and tart passion fruit is also fabulously nutritious. Passion fruit is full of vitamins A and C, fiber, minerals, and antioxidants. You know that you'll be treating your body well by drinking this colorful creation. This smoothie is a very nice drink to have on weekends with family and friends, so share a smoothie-making experience, have some good laughs, and create a couple of Mango Tango Smoothie dance moves. You'll just love the fun!

Time: 5 minutes | **Difficulty:** Easy | **Yields:** 16 ounces | **Serving size:** 8 ounces

1 cup ripe mango slices
1 cup chilled passion fruit pulp
Juice of ½ lemon
3 tablespoons raw honey
5 coconut water ice cubes

Place all ingredients in blender and blend on high until smooth.

NUTRITIONAL INFORMATION (PER SERVING SIZE):

CALORIES:	CARBOHYDRATES:	PROTEIN:	FAT:	SODIUM:	FIBER:	SUGAR:
235.5 (kcal)	58.1 (g)	4.1 (g)	0 (g)	258 (mg)	6 (g)	83 (g)

Passionate Raspberry Smoothie

When combined together, raspberries and passion fruit create a citrusy and sweet blast of goodness. Passion fruit is citrusy and tangy, while raspberries are sweet and tart; put the two together and you get a masterfully crafted blend with the best of both worlds. This truly delectable and magical drink quenches thirst and ends cravings. It's the perfect drink to wake up your senses in the morning and make you feel ready to attack all of the day's obstacles; it'll boost your energy and help kick-start your digestion too. It is also a wonderful drink to have with lunch or before lunch . . . a palate cleanser of sorts. So, have a glass of this Paleo smoothie before work or class. You'll find yourself coming back for more!

Time: 5 minutes | **Difficulty:** Easy | **Yields:** 16 ounces | **Serving size:** 8 ounces

1 cup frozen raspberries
1½ cups organic passion fruit juice
Juice of ½ lime
3 tablespoons raw honey
3 ice cubes

Place all ingredients in blender and blend on high until smooth.

NUTRITIONAL INFORMATION (PER SERVING SIZE):

CALORIES:	CARBOHYDRATES:	PROTEIN:	FAT:	SODIUM:	FIBER:	SUGAR:
225.25 (kcal)	49.5 (g)	1.25 (g)	0.5 (g)	4.5 (mg)	8 (g)	58 (g)

Paradise Beach Smoothie

What is green on the outside with a few soft thorns, and white on the inside with a few black seeds? Hint: It's a Latin American fruit that has a very unique shape and is usually used for juicing. Any guesses? It's typically bought in pulp form. No idea? It's the soursop! (It's also known as guanabana.) When used in a smoothie, soursop provides a fantastic creamy and smooth consistency, while also giving the drink a nice sweet and sour taste. This fruit is also full of great vitamins (like vitamin C), minerals (like calcium and phosphorus), and fiber, and can help boost your immune system and metabolism, relieve pain, increase energy, and help you maintain a healthy heart. Give this exotic Paleo smoothie a try! You'll love it.

Time: 5 minutes | **Difficulty:** Easy | **Yields:** 16 ounces | **Serving size:** 8 ounces

1 cup frozen blackberries
1½ cups chilled soursop (guanabana) pulp
2 tablespoons raw honey
3 ice cubes

Place all ingredients in blender and blend on high until smooth.

NUTRITIONAL INFORMATION (PER SERVING SIZE):

CALORIES:	CARBOHYDRATES:	PROTEIN:	FAT:	SODIUM:	FIBER:	SUGAR:
202.75 (kcal)	52.9 (g)	2.7 (g)	1 (g)	50 (mg)	19.13 (g)	84.7 (g)

Dragon Fruit Thrill Smoothie

This Dragon Fruit Thrill Smoothie is so delicious that once you start making them, you won't be able to stop! The delicious dragon fruit, locally called *pitahaya*, is native to South America. With its spiky skin, white insides, and little black seeds, it is truly an all-natural work of art that's beautifully unique, inside and out. Dragon fruit has three different varieties: one has red skin with white flesh; one has red skin with red flesh; and one has yellow skin with white flesh. Out of the three, the yellow dragon fruit seems to be the most popular in the Americas. Keep in mind that if you chose to use all of the fruit in a smoothie, you'll feel the seeds slightly, as you would with any berry.

Time: 5 minutes | **Difficulty:** Easy | **Yields:** 16 ounces | **Serving size:** 8 ounces

1 cup frozen blackberries
½ fresh dragon fruit
¼ cup canned coconut milk
1 cup unsweetened coconut milk (from carton, not canned)
2 tablespoons raw honey

Place all ingredients in blender and blend on high until smooth.

NUTRITIONAL INFORMATION (PER SERVING SIZE):

CALORIES:	CARBOHYDRATES:	PROTEIN:	FAT:	SODIUM:	FIBER:	SUGAR:
188.13 (kcal)	28.5 (g)	2.13 (g)	9.5 (g)	25.5 (mg)	9 (g)	43 (g)

Persimmon-ality Smoothie

This rich and creamy Paleo smoothie will make you crave a second serving, so be sure to keep lots of these ingredients in stock. This drink is high in potassium and vitamin A, making it a fantastic immune system booster and an aid for proper organ function. It uses persimmons, Japan's national fruit, as its main exotic ingredient, which is an easy ingredient to find in your local grocery stores. Just make sure you choose persimmons that are bright in color, plump, smooth, shiny, and have their leaf attached to them. You can store them at room temperature until they ripen, and refrigerate them after that for around three days. It's ideal for you to consume these when they are fully ripe, as they tend to be sweeter that way. You'll see them turn from green to orange while the ripening process happens, just like a tomato would. So make this great smoothie, kick back, and reap the fantastic health benefits!

Time: 5 minutes | **Difficulty:** Easy | **Yields:** 16 ounces | **Serving size:** 8 ounces

1 frozen banana
2 persimmons, leaves removed
1 cup unsweetened coconut milk (from carton, not canned)
¼ teaspoon vanilla extract
1 tablespoon maple syrup

Place all ingredients in blender and blend on high until smooth.

NUTRITIONAL INFORMATION (PER SERVING SIZE):

CALORIES:	CARBOHYDRATES:	PROTEIN:	FAT:	SODIUM:	FIBER:	SUGAR:
220.5 (kcal)	52.25 (g)	2.5 (g)	3.35 (g)	22 (mg)	16 (g)	69.5 (g)

Star Fruit Paradise Smoothie

It's yellow and it looks like a star. It's star fruit! Star fruit comes from a tree called the carambola, which is native to the Philippines and Southeast Asia. This tropical fruit is sweet (sometimes a bit sour), crisp, and very juicy—perfect for blending! In addition, this Paleo smoothie is packed with fiber to help with digestion; vitamin C, which is a natural antioxidant that fights against infectious agents; B-complex vitamins, that are great for all things related to the mind (mood, memory) and to boost your energy; and vitamin A, which is great for skin and eyesight. It's an overall great health booster that will definitely satisfy your sweet cravings. Also, in Brazil, star fruit is used as a diuretic and cough suppressant. It's very cool when good-tasting fruits have medicinal purposes, so mix one up and start feeling great!

Time: 5 minutes | **Difficulty:** Easy | **Yields:** 16 ounces | **Serving size:** 8 ounces

1 cup frozen mango slices
3 star fruits
1 cup orange juice, preferably freshly squeezed
1 teaspoon coconut cream concentrate
2 tablespoons raw honey

Place all ingredients in blender and blend on high until smooth.

NUTRITIONAL INFORMATION (PER SERVING SIZE):

CALORIES:	CARBOHYDRATES:	PROTEIN:	FAT:	SODIUM:	FIBER:	SUGAR:
197.5 (kcal)	46 (g)	4 (g)	1.5 (g)	7 (mg)	5 (g)	69 (g)

Guava Charm Smoothie

Did you know that the guava fruit is considered a superfood for its abundant antioxidants? And did you know that it contains even more vitamin C than oranges do? It is also very rich in fiber, potassium, and copper, which aid the body by regulating heart function and supporting important organs, bones, and tissue. This little fruit grows in tropical climates and is predominant in South America, Central America, Mexico, and Florida. Guavas are typically round, but sometimes you find some that are more on the oval side; its flesh has a pinkish tint to it, and its taste is usually sweet (depending on its ripeness). It is not a very hard fruit to find, so if you shop around for it (or even order it online) you can get a nice, fresh, ready-to-eat guava that is ready to be added to your Guava Charm Smoothie. If guava is new to you, try out this recipe and see how you like it!

Time: 5 minutes | **Difficulty:** Easy | **Yields:** 16 ounces | **Serving size:** 8 ounces

1 cup papaya chunks
2 ripe guavas
3 tablespoons raw honey
Juice of ½ lemon
1 cup coconut water ice cubes
¼ teaspoon ground ginger (to garnish)

1. Place all ingredients in blender, except for the ground ginger, and blend on high until smooth.
2. Pour smoothie in a glass and garnish with half of the ground ginger. Enjoy!

NUTRITIONAL INFORMATION (PER SERVING SIZE):

CALORIES:	CARBOHYDRATES:	PROTEIN:	FAT:	SODIUM:	FIBER:	SUGAR:
187.3 (kcal)	44.7 (g)	2.5 (g)	1 (g)	259.4 (mg)	6 (g)	67 (g)

Mango Passion Smoothie

Get ready for some tangy passion! This tasty and very tropical Mango Passion Smoothie will blow your mind. It is *that* good! It's rich, sweet, flavorful, citrusy, and packed with great nutrition, thanks to the passion fruit! This exotic ingredient is a fabulous source of fiber, protein, antioxidants, and iron. Also, every cup of passion fruit contains your daily dose of vitamin A, which is essential to maintain vigorous skin, good vision, and healthy cell reproduction. Go on and do your body a favor by drinking this great-tasting Paleo smoothie; you'll love how it tastes and how you'll feel.

Time: 5 minutes | **Difficulty:** Easy | **Yields:** 20 ounces | **Serving size:** 10 ounces

1 cup frozen mango slices
1 cup chilled passion fruit pulp
Juice of ½ lime
1 cup coconut water
2 tablespoons raw honey

Place all ingredients in blender and blend on high until smooth.

NUTRITIONAL INFORMATION (PER SERVING SIZE):

CALORIES:	CARBOHYDRATES:	PROTEIN:	FAT:	SODIUM:	FIBER:	SUGAR:
203.25 (kcal)	51.1 (g)	4.1 (g)	0 (g)	257.5 (mg)	6 (g)	65.5 (g)

Nothing Better Than Naranjilla Smoothie

This little gem is a great go-to drink when you're feeling like a sweet-and-sour treat that is low in calories. Don't let it trick you though! Even though this smoothie is lower in calories and fat, it has some great nutritional content! This Nothing Better Than Naranjilla Smoothie provides you with good amounts of potassium and calcium, which help you keep your bones strong and your brain and heart healthy. It's also a refreshing drink for those hot summer days, and is a wonderful accompaniment for lunch or dinner.

Time: 5 minutes | **Difficulty:** Easy | **Yields:** 16 ounces | **Serving size:** 8 ounces

1 cup chilled naranjilla pulp
1 cup coconut water
2 tablespoons raw honey
3 ice cubes

Place all ingredients in blender and blend on high until smooth.

NUTRITIONAL INFORMATION (PER SERVING SIZE):

CALORIES:	CARBOHYDRATES:	PROTEIN:	FAT:	SODIUM:	FIBER:	SUGAR:
102 (kcal)	25 (g)	1.5 (g)	0 (g)	254 (mg)	3 (g)	41 (g)

Playful Jackfruit Smoothie

Have you ever tried jackfruit? If not, you're in for a treat. Jackfruit is a very large fruit that grows in tropical climates such as Brazil, Southeast Asia, and India. Jackfruit is oval in shape, has thorny skin, and has soft flesh. It is a very good source of antioxidants, potassium, vitamins C and A, and carbohydrates, and will help boost your immune system, improve digestion, and give you superb skin. In addition, this smoothie will definitely calm your sweet tooth and give you lots of great energy. The combination of the sweet jackfruit taste and the wonderful punch of papaya and mango will have you jumping for joy!

Time: 5 minutes | **Difficulty:** Easy | **Yields:** 20 ounces | **Serving size:** 10 ounces

1 cup frozen mango slices
1 cup chopped jackfruit
½ cup ripe papaya chunks
½ cup unsweetened almond milk
2 tablespoons raw honey

Place all ingredients in blender and blend on high until smooth.

NUTRITIONAL INFORMATION (PER SERVING SIZE):

CALORIES:	CARBOHYDRATES:	PROTEIN:	FAT:	SODIUM:	FIBER:	SUGAR:
218.75 (kcal)	55 (g)	2 (g)	0.75 (g)	67 (mg)	5 (g)	63 (g)

Tomate de Árbol Smoothie

Tomate de árbol, or tamarillo, is a fruit that many people have not tried. While you may find this fruit difficult to find, it is found everywhere across South America. It is a shame this fruit isn't always readily available because it can help control high blood pressure and lower cholesterol, and it's packed with nutrients like vitamin A, phosphorus, potassium, iron, and calcium. Give Tomate de árbol a try in your Paleo smoothie. You'll really enjoy this South American treat!

Time: 5 minutes | **Difficulty:** Easy | **Yields:** 16 ounces | **Serving size:** 8 ounces

2 ripe tomates de árbol (tamarillos)
1 frozen banana
½ cup frozen blackberries
¾ cup orange juice, preferably freshly squeezed
2 tablespoons raw honey

1. Bring a small pot of water to a boil. Place tomates de árbol in boiling water for about 5 minutes; rinse in cold water and remove skin.
2. Place all ingredients in blender and blend on high until smooth.

NUTRITIONAL INFORMATION (PER SERVING SIZE):

CALORIES:	CARBOHYDRATES:	PROTEIN:	FAT:	SODIUM:	FIBER:	SUGAR:
200.3 (kcal)	50.65 (g)	1.52 (g)	0.35 (g)	3.5 (mg)	8.5 (g)	59.5 (g)

Orange Pineapple Smoothie

This healthy and exotic smoothie brings nothing but goodness to the table. The oranges, carrots, pineapples, and bananas provide you with a wonderful array of vitamins that will do wonders for your body—and they taste delicious when combined. But let's talk about the fresh ginger this recipe calls for. Freshly grated ginger gives a naturally spicy and aromatic flavor to your drink that is difficult to achieve with any other ingredient. This spice also contains potassium, which helps control your heart rate and blood pressure, as well as various essential oils like gingerol, an anti-inflammatory, painkilling, antibacterial, and nerve-soothing essential oil that helps promote a healthy digestive system. You're certain to feel fresh and renewed after drinking this fresh Paleo creation!

Time: 5 minutes | **Difficulty:** Easy | **Yields:** 16 ounces | **Serving size:** 8 ounces

1 cup frozen pineapple chunks
½ frozen banana
1 cup orange juice, preferably freshly squeezed
¼ cup freshly grated carrots
¼ teaspoon freshly grated ginger

Place all ingredients in blender and blend on high until smooth.

NUTRITIONAL INFORMATION (PER SERVING SIZE):

CALORIES:	CARBOHYDRATES:	PROTEIN:	FAT:	SODIUM:	FIBER:	SUGAR:
98.25 (kcal)	24.75 (g)	1.5 (g)	0 (g)	24.5 (mg)	6.5 (g)	33.5 (g)

Mango Soursop Smoothie

In this Paleo smoothie winner, the glorious soursop (also known as guanabana) is mixed with the beloved, juicy mango! These two ingredients will take you to a place of exotic wonder. All you have to do is take a sip, close your eyes, and pretend you're somewhere in a deep, green, and tropical Latin American jungle. Allow your taste buds to take you there; a place that knows no stress, no to-do lists, and no worries. Enjoy the wondrous citrusy and sweet flavors of these fruits, and know that while doing so you are also providing your body with essential vitamins and fiber to give yourself improved digestion, an immune system boost, and a healthy heart.

Time: 5 minutes | **Difficulty:** Easy | **Yields:** 16 ounces | **Serving size:** 8 ounces

1 cup frozen mango slices
1 cup chilled soursop (guanabana) pulp
½ cup coconut water
2 tablespoons raw honey

Place all ingredients in blender and blend on high until smooth.

NUTRITIONAL INFORMATION (PER SERVING SIZE):

CALORIES:	CARBOHYDRATES:	PROTEIN:	FAT:	SODIUM:	FIBER:	SUGAR:
203 (kcal)	52.25 (g)	2 (g)	0.5 (g)	23 (mg)	4.5 (g)	62 (g)

Blackberry Naranjilla Smoothie

Not a lot of Americans have tried the naranjilla, as it is a fruit particular to Ecuador and Colombia. But nothing beats the citrusy and tangy taste of this fruit; just thinking about it should make your mouth water! As far as taste goes, naranjilla resembles a cross between a pineapple and a lime. As far as looks go, the naranjilla fruit resembles a tomato, but with a very light orange color. How fun does this fruit sound? Once you try it, you will absolutely love it, especially when you pair it up with blackberries and sweet honey, like you do in this Paleo smoothie!

Time: 5 minutes | **Difficulty:** Easy | **Yields:** 16 ounces | **Serving size:** 8 ounces

1 cup frozen blackberries
1 cup chilled naranjilla pulp
Juice of 1 lemon
2 tablespoons raw honey

Place all ingredients in blender and blend on high until smooth.

NUTRITIONAL INFORMATION (PER SERVING SIZE):

CALORIES:	CARBOHYDRATES:	PROTEIN:	FAT:	SODIUM:	FIBER:	SUGAR:
116 (kcal)	30 (g)	1.5 (g)	0.5 (g)	3 (mg)	8 (g)	43 (g)

Peachy Lychee Smoothie

Meet the lychee. This attention-catching fruit has a leather-like pink peel that is unlike any other fruit out there. This fun fruit originated in Asia, but it is now also grown in Hawaii, Florida, and California. It's healthy, too! By eating just ½ cup of this fruit, you'll intake 113 percent of the Recommended Daily Value of vitamin C. It also has dietary fiber, antioxidants, and B-complex vitamins. When at the grocery store, try to pick up lychees that don't have any cuts and look fresh. Fresh lychees can last up to five weeks if kept refrigerated! Lychees are typically available in stores from July to October. Give this sweet-tasting fruit a try; you might find yourself feeling pretty exotic yourself!

Time: 5 minutes | **Difficulty:** Easy | **Yields:** 16 ounces | **Serving size:** 8 ounces

1 frozen banana
2 frozen lychees
½ cup frozen peach slices
½ cup frozen strawberries
1 cup orange juice, preferably freshly squeezed
Juice of ½ lime

Place all ingredients in blender and blend on high until smooth.

NUTRITIONAL INFORMATION (PER SERVING SIZE):

CALORIES:	CARBOHYDRATES:	PROTEIN:	FAT:	SODIUM:	FIBER:	SUGAR:
111 (kcal)	28.75 (g)	1.5 (g)	0 (g)	2.5 (mg)	7.5 (g)	27.5 (g)

APPENDIX
Metric Conversion Chart

VOLUME CONVERSIONS	
U.S. Volume Measure	**Metric Equivalent**
⅛ teaspoon	0.5 milliliter
¼ teaspoon	1 milliliter
½ teaspoon	2 milliliters
1 teaspoon	5 milliliters
½ tablespoon	7 milliliters
1 tablespoon (3 teaspoons)	15 milliliters
2 tablespoons (1 fluid ounce)	30 milliliters
¼ cup (4 tablespoons)	60 milliliters
⅓ cup	90 milliliters
½ cup (4 fluid ounces)	125 milliliters
⅔ cup	160 milliliters
¾ cup (6 fluid ounces)	180 milliliters
1 cup (16 tablespoons)	250 milliliters
1 pint (2 cups)	500 milliliters
1 quart (4 cups)	1 liter (about)
WEIGHT CONVERSIONS	
U.S. Weight Measure	**Metric Equivalent**
½ ounce	15 grams
1 ounce	30 grams
2 ounces	60 grams
3 ounces	85 grams
¼ pound (4 ounces)	115 grams
½ pound (8 ounces)	225 grams
¾ pound (12 ounces)	340 grams
1 pound (16 ounces)	454 grams

Index

About the Author

Mariel Lewis is the writer and recipe developer behind the popular blog AmazingPaleo.com. She is a health and fitness enthusiast from Quito, Ecuador, who currently resides in Boise, Idaho. Her love for the (healthier) culinary arts began during her college years when she experimented with various cuisines. It wasn't until three years after her culinary journey began and through much research that she discovered the infinite benefits of the Paleolithic diet. Ever since, she has spent countless hours in the kitchen creating delicious Paleo recipes.